The Missing Revolution

A manifesto of future spirituality

Shai Tubali

Published by Crusader eBooks, Perth, Western Australia

Typesetting, Layout and Cover Design by eBooks West

Boy and Kite cover image from *http://wallpapers-place.com*

Copyright © Shai Tubali 2013

The right of Shai Tubali to be identified as author of this work has been asserted by him in accordance with the provisions of the Australian Copyright Act 1968.

All rights reserved. Without limiting the rights under copyright reserved above, no part of this publication may be reproduced in any form by any means without the prior written permission of the copyright owner.

National Library of Australia Cataloguing-in-Publication entry

Author: Tubali, Shai, author.

Title: The missing revolution: a manifesto of future spirituality /Shai Tubali.

ISBN: 978-0-9872987-9-9 (paperback)

Subjects: Spiritual life.

Dewey Number: 291.4

CONTENTS

Chapter One: The Missing Revolution — 1

Chapter Two: When East Does Not Meet West — 15

Chapter Three: The Illusion of Emptiness — 30

Chapter Four: The Psychological Trap — 43

Chapter Five: The Death of the Guru — 58

Chapter Six: A Pre-modern Ghost — 73

Chapter Seven: The Call — 90

Chapter Eight: A Stand in the World — 107

Chapter Nine: The Dark Side of the Western Spirit — 123

Chapter Ten: Whatever Happened to Logic? — 140

Chapter Eleven: The Great March of Evolution — 157

Chapter Twelve: Our Credo — 175

Chapter One:

The Missing Revolution

Among many other revolutions, the 20th century has brought forth the great revolution of the New Age movement: a new Western spirituality which - inspired by the Eastern traditions, the weakening of mainstream religions, the birth of the psychologically free individual, and the rise of great teachers who mixed East and West - has managed to develop a far more autonomous, independent and direct contact with the higher reality.

But nowadays, so it seems, this revolution has sunk into a comfortable middle class oblivion. Why doesn't it evolve further into its bolder, more enlightening and liberating stages? Where did we get stuck and what can we do in order to re-awaken and strengthen this great spirit?

This manifesto draws the outlines of both the crisis and the challenge of the New Age movement, offering a way out and up - towards an authentic and mature Western spirituality for the 21st century.

The 20th century was indeed a tremendous turning point for the Western spiritual world. The influx of Eastern spiritual masters, who came from India, Tibet, China and other countries, has permanently reshaped the Western view on spirituality; what used to be only glimpses of influence in the 19th century became a mass movement. Great teachers such as Vivekananda (who appeared in the West just at the end of the 19th century), Jiddu Krishnamurti, Yogananda, Sivananda, Muktananda, Osho, Maharishi Mahesh Yogi, the 14th Dalai Lama, Chogyam Trungpa, D.T. Suzuki - and many, many others - introduced to the West the teachings of Yoga, Tantra, Buddhism, Zen-Buddhism, Taoism and perhaps most importantly, the notion of spiritual enlightenment or liberation.

Many in the West, who were torn between the residues of the monotheistic religions and the rising of secular individualism, found much solace in the Eastern spiritual ideas and practices. Being so weary of the remote father-figure of God and the indirectness of the somewhat awkward religious commandments and laws, they sought for a much more direct and inner approach, which can simultaneously support their ever-growing individualism and their quest for the naked truth of life.

The Eastern teachings were exactly what they needed: they served as a missing link which could connect the individual autonomy with the greater force of life. Slowly but surely these teachings forced even monotheistic religious thought out of its heavy symbolism and dogmatic structures and led it towards understanding that if it ever wished to survive in the 20th century, it would have to make itself relevant and useful for the new evolving brain. Religious superstitions, accompanied by an irrational demand to simply 'believe', could not suffice anymore. What we can observe today as the universal Kabala teachings or the much more available Christian thought, could have never taken place without the powerful influence of Eastern thinking.

The 20th century was, in this sense, a great point of intersection between the weakening of religious thought and practice, the birth of the free individual, the Eastern teachings and the rising of more integrative teachers, who were quick to realize the implications of the union between East and West. These later kind of teachers – such as Jiddu Krishnamurti, Osho and Gurdjieff – were extremely sharp and brilliant in understanding that in the West we do not need the crutches of any kind of religious authority or mediating tradition; we must stand alone as real individuals, find the divine within us and be the divine ourselves. 'There is no power outside of man', stated UG Krishnamurti, and this saying actually quite sums up this entirely new philosophy: spiritual enlightenment is really the key for the birth of a new and truly independent kind of human being.

This tremendous revolution in our spiritual understanding was not very different from other revolutions in the 20th century. In Physics and Cosmology, Einstein deconstructed the absolute time and space, and brought about, unintentionally, the randomness and uncertainties of quantum physics; in philosophy, Nietzsche called for the death of God and initiated both the rising of a genuine secular individuality and the post-modern, deconstructive way of thinking; in Psychology, Freud re-created the human psyche as a totally internal arena in which inner forces of the subconscious give shape to our behavior and actions; in literature, Joyce and Proust demolished all literary certainties of the 19th century; abstract painting and atonal music were inevitable too. Indeed, the greatest intellectual enterprise of the 20th century was to deconstruct all absolutes and all external forces; we realized the internalness of the universe, that the universe is not embedded in some outer and absolute being-in-itself but that it is in fact objectively-godless and completely workable in terms of natural and human evolution alone. Truth is no longer an outside and indifferent eternal presence – it is to be found within the universe, within its molecules and the delicate subatomic structures.

The mechanical, absolute, Newtonic order, which clearly defined physics, music, art, philosophy and psychology crashed into relativity. Everything was influenced, including spiritual thought. This was actually the birth of the New Age movement, which its essential notion is that 'God (or the divine) is within my own self'. The dual separation, which the Western religions have managed to maintain so well, couldn't survive this great collapse of all absolutes and externals into the evolving universe. The New Age movement drew all forces into the internal domain; God has become a state of consciousness rather than a someone; the divine law has transformed into internal observation and a process of inner revolution; waiting for divine grace has changed its direction and has finally become a total responsibility for our own suffering and ignorance and also an understanding that our own behavior and actions are the only real potential source of grace.

Yes, even for us, in the New Age movement - and we're all part of it as long as we engage in a secular, independent and individual spirituality -

God is dead. Of course, nothing substantial really died in this process; it is only a notion, a misguided assumption of absolutism that died, and we are left with a much more non-dualist perception of the Godhead. This perception implies a greater responsibility along with a greater energy that is being pumped up into the individual self. In a way, the moment God died, we became the Godhead; no external force can ever save us from now on, as this freedom also means a frightening aloneness.

Are we aware of this entire revolution, which we are all part of? Do we realize that we are the holders of the key for the new Western spirituality? Do we understand what we did and what the implications of this great achievement are? Since part and parcel of the New Age neurosis is the inability, and even the proud refusal, to observe our own process in objective terms and to analyze it as part of the grand, external human evolution, it is usually very hard for us to seriously consider this large-scale revolution, let alone our active involvement in it.

We gave birth to an independent, individual, secular, non-dual Western spirituality. This spirituality draws its strength from both the gifts of the East and the extrication of the inner wisdom from the great past-traditions of the West. More unconsciously, we also draw our strength from Freud and Nietzsche, from Einstein and, yes, even Darwin. We have undone divine grace and we have assimilated God into our own consciousness. We have demolished belief and replaced it with responsibility and self-authority. Spirituality has become an inner realm, which requires no belief but direct communion - this is, after all, the entire fundamental idea of meditation (as opposed to prayer, for example). Our New Age spirituality demands total liberation from all externals, including external spiritual authorities and mediators, laws and commandments, reward and punishment and so on. It claims our ability to save ourselves through the power of our own consciousness, since the center of gravity, responsibility and leadership has moved into the very center of the human spirit.

But have we declared it - consciously, lucidly, boldly? Has this become a cornerstone of something else? Not at all. In fact, ever since this great influx of spiritual passion has given birth to the New Age movement, it seems that all we do is entrench ourselves somewhere in the distant margins of the world. We are dispersed, weak and self-consumed. Our voice is not heard anywhere. But why is this so? Is it because the spiritual life is by its very nature apathetic to the world of time and space, arrogantly looking down at it from the eternal realms of the spirit? Is it because we have completely misunderstood what we did, confusing individuality with narcissism and self-authority with self-obsession? Or is it because we simply do our best to shirk this heavy burden of responsibility, trying to evade the complex implications which, first and foremost, demand a new Western, highly-developed interpretation of spirituality for the 21th century?

My strong feeling is that it is time for us to have a spirituality of our own. This is the next necessary step, while we continually procrastinate. Indeed, this is a great paradigm shift and we all ought to be brave and thorough in pushing it further. But the thing is that as long as we don't do it, we are doomed to be wandering from one world to another without much sense in anything we do. And why is that? This is because we, as the Western spiritual adherents, live just on the borderline between matter and spirit, East and West, past and future, science and religion, secular individualism and the ancient God-father, absolutism and relativism. We haven't chosen yet, consciously, this specific form of life. Being a spiritual Westerner implies living in a world of becoming and evolving, achieving and progressing; it means partaking in a certain mentality and spirit of change and movement, but more than that, it means *embracing* the world of change and movement.

As the New Agers it seems that we haven't chosen this world at all, so we live on the periphery, trying to remain untouched and totally avoiding our role in it. It is as if we try to live the other pole of its mentality and spirit, while still living here somehow. Yet trying to live here, in the West, *and* to pursue a totally opposite spirit seems to be the cause of suffering for many of us. We do our best to deny the world in a place which by its very nature embraces the world and is driven to live it through.

What I claim here is that we do not *step in*. This way we remain an insignificant minority, while to me it seems that we are destined to hand on the keys of the next human evolution. We make ourselves invisible, instead of joyfully continuing to develop the major breakthrough of the New Age movement.

This manifesto is inspired by one single troubled question: where are we really? Where did we get stuck? Why don't we become a genuine part of the history of the world? Why don't we leave an impact anywhere around? Why is it that our presence is so weak, while our responsibility is to translate the new spiritual wisdom into a world-changing immense presence? Why don't we gather and enthusiastically ask ourselves: what is our purpose and destiny as a world movement?

By agreeing to live in the periphery we are hurting both ourselves and the world at large. We simply avoid our true nature, which its first sign is a fully involved and participative spirit. To be a yogi in a cave is certainly not our spirituality, and yet we hide in our Western, comfortable, middle class caves. But we are still here for a reason, are we not? Something keeps us in here, some sort of a question mark which is ideally meant to show us the way.

This book was written in 2012, which many in the New Age movement have impatiently waited for, as if something cosmic should drop down from the sky and miraculously change us all. But this is exactly the opposite of *real* New Age, which understands that the only revolution that could ever take place is the one that we might choose to create, as there's no power outside of man and no major changes apart from conscious human choices.

Chapter Two:

When East Does Not Meet West

How the inspiration of the great teaching of the East has become twisted along the way and has turned into a source of confusion for us in the West.

> "The wise seeker knows: the fruit of my endeavors will be commensurate with the intensity of my self-effort, and neither fate nor a god can ordain it otherwise"
>
> [Yoga Vasishta, ancient Hindu scripture]

The Gifts

Before anything else, we must discuss one of the major influences on the New Age culture: the Eastern traditions. Squeezing together Hinduism, Yoga, Tantra, Buddhism, Tibetan-Buddhism, Zen-Buddhism, Taoism and some other minor traditions, into one world-view is a gross generalization, and yet, it seems to me that there is some overall spirit which underlies them all. This overall spirit, as I already mentioned in the introductory chapter, started blowing towards the West at the end of the 19th century and attained its highest influential power somewhere in the midst of the 20th century.

The greatest gift of Eastern spirituality is, first and foremost, its liberating directness. Unlike the Western monotheistic religions, this kind of spirituality - at least, the way it has been presented to the West during the 20th century - is not heavily masked and concealed by metaphors, symbols and the general hesitation of the god-fearing theologist. It does not demand faith without a proof, a structured and rigid set of laws and commandments and even not the slightest form of relationship with some God-father.

The Eastern spiritual philosophy deals with the liberation of the individual consciousness and with the conditions for its realization. It is about claiming our right to experience a union with the divine consciousness or with the wholeness of life and the cosmos; it is all about the understanding that 'I' and 'That' are essentially one and the same; it is a finger which boldly points at the seeking subject as the final goal of all seeking. And the most awesome thing about it is that this is not even a philosophy to consider and embrace, but rather a naked inner truth which one can verify only through direct inner experience. In fact, at the very heart of these traditions lies the *demand* for direct experience as the foundation of the entire philosophical structure. Naturally, the emphasis of this kind of spirituality is on meditation, which is basically about creating the right setting for the mind to realize a truth that lies beyond its known frontiers and that evades all familiar structures of religious practice.

Indeed, this was a tremendous influence on the accelerating development of the New Age movement during the 20th century. It has completely transformed the image of God into a state of consciousness, thus turning the Godhead into an inward phenomenon which is destined to burst out of the individual consciousness as a higher level of self-identification. At once, religion was no longer needed; one could search within oneself and actually fulfill the basic religious longing, which is to communicate with the higher power. This does not mean that this level of inner recognition has never occurred in Western spiritual cultures, either in core-groups within the context of the great religions or in rare individuals, but even then it was usually wrapped in symbols and religious terminology. One way or the other, it is clear that as a global movement the Western spiritual culture desperately needed an awakening of this kind of spirit, and that only through the Eastern large wave which covered its shores, could it ever attain this level of tuning and focus.

The Eastern traditions have always excelled in the diligent mapping of the inner territories of human consciousness. Patiently, for thousands of years their seers drew careful outlines of our subtle anatomies, maps for the expansion of consciousness, stages of development towards final liberation and accurate inner roadmaps for the inner journey, obstacles and traps included. In a way, they developed a systematic science of consciousness, which is unprecedented in the history of the world.

So these were the gifts which the Eastern spirit has bestowed upon us: the centrality of meditation in spiritual practice (the notion of direct experience); the divine self-identity (the notion of non-duality), and the detailed maps of human consciousness (the notion of a gradual advance towards final realization). This definitely sounds great! But what went wrong along the way? Somehow the spirit of the East has been twisted and abused and has eventually damaged the young evolving spirit of the New Age movement. Our inability to extricate the depths of this spirit out of the external traditional structures has turned it into what now seems as a dangerous superficiality. The sad result: an ongoing cultural decay.

The Problems

There have been at least three major problems in assimilating the Eastern spirit into our Western spirituality. In this latter part of this chapter I shall focus on the first one.

First of all, we have extracted from the Eastern wisdom only the superficial layers of the teachings, while carelessly abandoning the much more complex and demanding layers. All liberation teachings of the East are endowed with great depth, great seriousness and great demand from the individual seeker. Somehow, this has totally lost along the way, leaving us with empty slogans, mediocre teachings, blurred distinctions and very unjustified spiritual pride.

Perhaps the general Western tendency for consumerism and copywriting is to blame, but to me it seems that there is a much deeper cause: it is the fear of the challenges of Western life, which lurks within the very heart of the New Age members – a fear that drives us towards a total reaction to the Western spirit. Since the Western spirit is all about becoming and achieving, advancing and changing, we, who couldn't bear this heavy yoke, had desperately sought for the very opposite until we found it in the form of the Eastern wisdom: if the Western spirit revolves around effort, we will react with 'total effortlessness'; if it encourages achievements, we will define ourselves as 'non-achievers'; we will look only for that which never changes, since the only right response for the anxiety-ridden movement of the West is, of course, a *total and absolute rest*.

This somewhat childish reaction, which is rooted in deep fear and general sense of inadequacy, has led us to negating the tremendous complexity and paradoxical knowledge of the East. For example, while the Eastern teachings present a great demand for effort and diligence - in fact, some of the more profound teachings clearly state that the entire achievement of liberation *totally* depends on self-effort* - most Eastern-inspired teachings in the West put much emphasis on instant enlightenment - getting it in one glimpse or brief moment; claiming that 'the less you do, the closer you get', and childishly denying the notion of a gradual process. Driven by a compulsion to resist the Western challenge, they flatten the ancient wisdoms, thus withholding the possibility for many to actually evolve towards a stabilized stage of development.

What is usually referred to as the 'Satsang culture' is a good example for both the reactive New Age movement and the horrible flattening of the great ancient wisdoms. Although it is indeed very relieving and liberating to firmly negate all frameworks and structures and leaving only the naked truth, it is still alarming to realize that many people are conditioned to think that self-effort, gradual advance and perpetual self-overcoming are not part of spiritual transformation and that in a way they even oppose it. We have quite forgotten that in spite of our ability to intellectually assimilate the idea of the internal or subjective God, actually attaining and embodying this realization is a matter of a radical evolutionary achievement. Probably we tend to ignore the fact that truly liberated human beings are still extremely rare: several dozen, at the most.

Indeed, nowadays only a few teachers will adhere to the ancient knowledge which explicitly distinguishes between *initial awakening* or the beginning phase of the awakening of Kundalini and *final liberation* (Jivanmukti - liberated while still in the body). In the absence of such a clear distinction, many who claim to be 'enlightened' are truly only awakened, but lacking in the profound teaching's road signs they fully content themselves with their attainment, and thus withhold the further flow of this blessed evolutionary process. In popular literature dealing with 'enlightenment' the emphasis is on the initial moment of release, which traditionally characterizes the first combustion of the Kundalini fire. To actually complete the process is truly a very uncommon attainment, and the great differences between awakened teachers and liberated teachers may testify to that.

Slowly but surely we have replaced the detailed maps, the gradual evolution and the tremendous self-effort with shallow experiences and unexpected graceful moments. A constant process of reduction erodes the immaculate teachings: an enthusiastic Westerner goes to a great Yogi, and after being slightly initiated by him, he hurriedly goes to spread the word and to give his blessing to very short-lived experiences and revelations; then these blessed ones go to teach and 'recognize' even lesser attainments. Eventually, the understanding of what enlightenment really is becomes so foggy and misty that no one really knows what they're talking about. Everything sounds the same; all hierarchical knowledge and razor-sharp distinctions are lost in the process.

It is a pity because the encounter between the Eastern science of consciousness and the Western scientific and systematic inclination could have yielded a tremendous breakthrough: there could have been a genuine and marvelous continuum of growing knowledge, which should have culminated in a highly realistic and evolutionary understanding of enlightenment. After all, the Western mind is extraordinary in its ability to embrace complexity. More than that, it is very questionable that we should have a Satsang scene at all – is it really authentic in our Western culture? Doesn't it become a cheap imitation of something that only in its right cultural context seems to be in place? What is natural in the East is not necessarily natural for us, and the implication of this insight is that we still do not possess the correct platform for the highest, most radical New Age teachings. The right platform mustn't be based on a childish reaction - it must grow from within the great Western philosophical lineage.

Driven by the fear of the harshness of Western's constant movement, we have been psychologically attracted mainly towards the feminine aspects of the Eastern traditions: complete acceptance and effortless 'flow'; being absorbed in internal processes rather than being involved in the world; being passive and receptive instead of pro-actively moving through life. We have been so inclined towards these aspects, due to our psychological fears, that we have somehow completely fooled ourselves to believing that this is what the Eastern teaching is all about. We have elegantly neglected the harder, more masculine parts of this wisdom: the tremendous struggle - yes, struggle! - for liberation, the intellectual complexity that is filled with paradoxical guidance and puzzling contradictions, and the level of ambition which is clearly required for spiritual transformations. For some reason, we have put great emphasis on relieving notions such as the 'here and now' - mere fragments of sophisticated teachings - as if spiritual practice was only ever meant to serve as a pain-killer for escapist Westerners. This also manifests in the 'Satsang culture', as a deceptive invitation to find rest and eternal peace without any friction whatsoever, which are basically another way to put ourselves to sleep.

The spiritual transformation in the West, so I believe, must be met with a corresponding wakeful Western mind. Uniting with the Eastern gifts, it can realize liberation as a new evolutionary stage, which can actually better embrace the world of change. Combining the scientific Western spirit with the Eastern science of consciousness, it will definitely and wholeheartedly appreciate the masculine parts of these traditions, since they are not that far from the Western spirit: conscious effort, ambition, active engagement, razor-sharp distinctions, evolutionary tension and a profound longing for advancement. The West *genuinely* meets the East not at the point of complete rest but rather at the point of self-effort. The passive, feminine aspects of the East are acutely insufficient in the Western world, and are also harming for our evolving New Age movement.

* See the masterful 'Yoga Vasishta', for example.

Chapter Three:

The Illusion of Emptiness

How we have mistakenly embraced the emptiness of the East and twisted the notion of the divine self in order to escape Western life

> "Linguistic danger to spiritual freedom. — Every word is a prejudice".
>
> [Friedrich Nietzsche, philosopher]

The excited yet restrained audience slowly takes its seat on the few dozen meditation chairs and mattresses. Then, readily, everybody closes their eyes, awaiting the elusive presence of the teacher to appear. In the dimmed room, lit up only by some gentle candles, the teacher finally arrives, clothed solely in white, his face serene and his eyes penetrating. When he sits, he eye-gazes everyone softly, smiles a mysterious smile, folds his hands for a long Hindu 'Namaste' gesture and then begins to speak, even to whisper, about the nature of silence. The people listen with intense quietude, accompanied by a tensed and romantic expectation to collide with some sudden insight which will simply 'change everything', first and foremost - some great understanding that will immediately wipe away all sorrow. The teacher goes on speaking, actually quoting all the known clichés of the Satsang scene - most of the people in the audience could have said it themselves in quite the same elegance - but anyway everybody knows that truth is eternal and that there's actually nothing to say. A silence prevails in the room, signaling that there is a truth in the air, but somehow this silence is lifeless and barren and has nothing to do with life as we know it; it verges on some twilight zone in which the difference between liberation and fleeing life into some relieving sanctuary is not clear anymore.

As I pointed out in the previous chapter, the Satsang scene is a good example for the misuse of the Eastern spirit - precisely because this scene aspires to represent the 'jewel in the crown', the living heart of the Eastern knowledge. We have unwisely utilized the teachings of the East, partly because the effort to copy it into the West has been superficial, and partly because large portions of these teachings are simply irrelevant in a Western culture (sometimes they even take an absurd and grotesque form, because of this awkward imitation).

A large part of the confusion is caused by the effort to force the Western mind with its increasing complexity into the Eastern view of reality. What works pretty well for the Eastern mind cannot, and should not, fit the Western's thought structures. An intelligent act would have been to extract exactly what we need from the Eastern wisdom and leave *everything else* behind.

As I already mentioned, we desperately need the knowledge of the pure subject for the further evolution of the autonomous individual; we also need meditation and accurate maps of the evolution of human consciousness. Yet we must learn how to use these gifts wisely, otherwise we get caught in trying to succumb to a spiritual world-view which doesn't fit us at all and thus we suffer, consciously and unconsciously.

So this is exactly what the other two major problems point at - our submission to the anti-Western world-views, especially the ones which emphasize emptiness and self-annihilation or 'liberation from life'.

Usually in the New Age movement we give little regard to the implications of the words we use, as if the truth, being anyway elusive, can be somehow transmitted energetically. But every word we choose radically shapes our minds and thus gives specific direction for our life and deeds.

The choice of so many of us to embrace terms like 'emptiness', 'nothingness', 'infinite space' and 'stillness' as the preferred pointers of reality, inevitably leads to a profound negation of the valid existence of the world. After all, the mere *feeling* of these words evokes the cool and indifferent touch of the spirit. A world-view that negates the existence of the world of time and space, and bluntly considers it as an 'illusion', may be suitable for the East, but it certainly does not make any sense in the West.

We have to understand that the Eastern spirit is biased by its inclination towards the inner, subjective world; the realm of the spirit contains much more reality while the world of phenomena pales into insignificance. Although there is a major difference between 'Nirvana' or 'Liberation' and the monotheistic notion of the superiority of the spirit over the flesh - the 'other world' is external while Nirvana is internal and also the 'other world' is only after the body perishes and Nirvana can occur within the physical body - the Eastern spirit is clearly characterized by its far-distance gaze towards the heavens of the subjective realms and by its infatuation with transcending the objective world.

Too often in the New Age movement we make a sincere effort to adopt the world-negating world-view and to live the emptiness or infinite space in the midst of the Western life. We're developing a longing for non-creation, for devolution, a strange state in which one passionately regresses back to the pure spirit before the big bang. But why? Isn't that the most anti-Western approach we can ever embrace? Most fundamentally, it nourishes our fear of life and hinders our capacity to love life. An external or internal renunciation of the world can easily conceal escapist tendency caused by psychological instability. If somebody wants to renounce the world, why should he stay in the midst of the Western life? We cannot live in totality as long as we are torn between the renunciation within us and the Westerner within us - being torn, we do not excel in living neither of these two possibilities. We have to choose one day, and considering 'emptiness' as absolute reality definitely won't help us in this choice.

We must understand that the Eastern spirituality tends to empty the content of this universe, to tag it as 'the passing and relative world of phenomena' and to turn its back on it for the sake of the purity of the subjective world. By emptying the universe from its content and labeling it with blurry terms, these spiritual doctrines dull and stupefy our mind. This may be suitable for the East, but in the West removing the entire universe from the equation of reality is simply invalid.

Perhaps a better term for us could be 'fullness' - a multi-layered fullness, which can include both the transcendental and the process of evolution and becoming as *different layers* of the absolute reality. Often in the Satsang culture speakers follow the notion of non-duality, but the Eastern non-duality is for us dual by its very nature: it distinguishes reality from the world of time and space. Isn't it time for us to realize that the Western spirituality must develop its own type of non-duality - a spirit that fully embraces as reality the world of change and the entire unfolding universe? This kind of spirituality springs from the heart of the universe, and doesn't roam somewhere outside the visible worlds.

This act of fusion matches greatly the philosophical continuum of the Western spirit. By giving a reality tag to the universe we bring God or reality into the universe; the center of divine gravity moves into the very heart of matter. This is much more than a philosophical shift, for this understanding implies that to be spiritual means to be involved and fully engaged in the world.

Another complementary idea is 'self-annihilation' or the disappearance of the 'ego'. The fact that the 'ego' is borrowed from the psychological tradition of the West is quite intriguing. Again, as with emptiness and stillness, using this notion in the West is hazardous, and childish; it's like going against a tremendous evolutionary achievement and wanting to regress to some prehistoric stage in which we had no ego. In a Western context this sounds like madness. In Western thought, the ego can become perhaps an evolutionary layer on which another layer may be added - because in the West we become more and more complex, and never less complex. A more mature version of this can be the expansion of the self, an expansion which inevitably includes the ego and recognizes its importance.

Along with 'self-annihilation' comes the notion of final liberation from the cycle of life and death. In the Eastern traditions, life is often considered to be synonymous with suffering, and liberation means being excused from the vicious cycle of birth and re-birth. Again, these teachings might support our psychological fear and even hatred of life, and they can easily become a haven for those who cannot cope (or don't feel like coping). In the West, in cultivating longing to escape life we support unconscious wishes which take the form of subtle suicide.

The very notion of self-redemption turns in the West into pure escapism. This kind of idea consists in a major part in the narcissistic, self-observant and self-indulgent typical character of New Age followers. The emphasis on a subjective world - giving it a higher value of reality compared to an objective world - leads us to entrenching ourselves more and more in a protected bunker which powerfully filters all messages from the external world.

The pure self has become another form of avoidance, just like liberation and self-dissolution. Meditation for too many is only a relieving sanctuary in which they can forget for some time the pressing burdens of this world. So here, again, perhaps we should replace 'liberation from the world' with 'liberation *for* the world': a freedom from psychological bondage which makes us fully available for the world.

Lastly, we should also include in this terminological revolution the terms 'surrender', 'devotion' and 'giving in to the higher power of life or God'. These terms are completely intertwined with remaining Eastern world-views: since reality is emptiness and the objective world is nothing but a passing and relative realm, we must realize this illusion, let go of the ego that binds us to this world and liberate ourselves from the need to come back to the visible realm.

One of the major practices for self-annihilation is, naturally, surrendering and allowing everything to flow just as it is, while smiling quietly to ourselves and knowing that this is merely the play of God and so on.

This mythology, which is completely derived from Eastern mysticism, may sound relieving, but it is not Western in any way and it is dangerous for the Western mind. It cultivates passivity and impotence, and in that encourages a general sense of apathy. Perhaps we could replace 'surrender' with 'co-creating' as a middle solution between the over-masculine fire of the West and the over-feminine cool waters of the East. After all, there is no true need to 'flow in life' in the submissive way of faint surrender and squashing our will; the term may equally point at the healthy growing capacity to respond to life's challenges out of freedom and inner stability.

These are just suggestions, but the basic realization is not a suggestion but a necessity: we must destroy the Eastern concepts that have been deeply implanted in us and turned into limiting conditioning. Otherwise, we will get caught forever in this state of alienation, which constantly erodes our healthy energies of will, passion and involvement through the irrelevant ideas of nothingness and illusion, self-annihilation and total flow, divine will and silent and distant spiritual arrogance.

Chapter Four:

The Psychological Trap

The good and the bad effects of the psychological revolution on the New Age movement* Read how this revolution has equipped us with great keys for liberation, yet has also entrapped our mind in overwhelming narcissism and hypersensitivity.

> "No new beliefs, no new paradigm, no new myths, no new ideas, will staunch the encroaching anguish. Not a new belief for the self, but the transcendence of the self altogether, is the only path that avails".
>
> [Ken Wilber, philosopher]

The psychological revolution, which began with Freud, was (and still is) another major influence on the New Age culture. One can easily understand the connection between the birth of a non-religious, autonomous and individual spirituality and the Freudian movement: the psychological revolution has marked the beginning of individual psychotherapy, which consequently gave rise to a new capacity for self-analysis and deeper self-understanding of the forces within ourselves; this kind of new capacity immediately implied a strengthened sense of personal sovereignty.

The birth of an individual psychology has also marked the internalization of many forces which until then seemed to be external. What used to be thought of as demons and angels became all at once a world of inner forces which are the ones to determine the structures of our personality. When all psychological forces lose their traditional mystification, we are finally able to realize that 'there is no power outside of man', and therefore this can be the beginning of self-responsibility and total sovereignty. Creating and untying psychological suffering are always only in our hands, and depend on our own ignorance or understanding.

The scientific recognition of the existence of the subconscious, enabled by Freud, was probably the greatest leap of them all. The notion of subtle layers of the psyche, which give shape in the dark to our visible patterns of behavior and worldviews, and the notion of repression that naturally follows it, have equipped us with a fuller insight into the structures of our own psyche and a better capacity to become the masters of our own inner world.

Ideally, this great contribution should have bestowed on the New Age movement some very important keys. First and foremost, an independent and liberating understanding of our innermost structures which can support the essential idea of liberation through the power of our own consciousness, and the resulting growing capacity to withstand the simultaneous demand for spiritual transformation and managing the complex challenges of the Western world.

But this tendency to self-analysis has been acutely misused by the New Age movement. This movement, more than other streams of human culture, suffers a psychological weakness that makes it vulnerable to turning self-analysis into obsession. So let us follow in Freud's footsteps for a moment and examine the unconscious hidden motives which bring about the inclination in the New Age movement towards the psychological practice of self-observation and self-diagnosis.

What lies in the very foundation of so many beliefs and behaviors of our New Age culture is a general sense of inadequacy and inability to cope; a deep-rooted fear which gives rise to the feeling of not belonging to this world. In a way, the New Age movement attracts so many who unconsciously seek for ways to avoid and to flee Western challenges - people who feel they simply cannot handle the pressure. The New Age worldview, with its reassuring messages and practices, offers them not only solace and refuge but even a psychological protective mechanism of patronization, looking down on everyone else, and an illusory sense of power. In this way, the powerless become powerful in their own eyes, just like in Nietzsche's 'slave morality'.

In more esoteric terms, which will be further developed in this manifesto, the fragility and vulnerability of this movement's three lower chakras give rise to a false spirituality: some twisted form of an escapist mass movement which constantly nurtures with 'concepts' and 'inner experiences' its own neurosis. Only if we manage to fortify our collective three lower chakras can we create a truly capable self - stable, independent and powerful - on which an authentic spirituality might gradually evolve; a spirituality that really doesn't need to escape anything.

So what happens when we combine an escapist tendency with an increased capacity for self-analysis? That's right: we get a deeper self-entrenching; one tirelessly observes oneself instead of actually acting in the world, thus a quality which was destined to help us become more awake, responsible and engaged, has helped us instead to escape life in more sophisticated ways. The psychological view has only made it worse for the New Age movement: ironically, it backs us up with more excuses for our self-impotence instead of aiding us in the important task of standing on our own feet. As we constantly dig within ourselves to trace hidden traumas, unconscious motives and psychological patterns, we unknowingly become more narcissistic, and more hyper-sensitive. Analyzing ourselves forever does not free us. In fact it makes us delve within ourselves without ever being able to be fully released into the world. It also enhances our emotionalism, since we give a tremendous attention to 'feelings' as if they were the real spiritual center of our being, and the indication of our true self.

The strange mixture of feminine Eastern notions such as 'here and now' or 'go with the flow' and this introverted self-wallowing has turned our gaze completely towards the subjective realms. We became childish and vulnerable. No firm stand can ever develop in such castrating conditions; instead, one observes the world from the bunker of emotions and self-observation. We sink deeper into ourselves, since we lack the real drive that can use the knowledge of the subconscious for a liberating leap.

A narcissistic self-observation doesn't mean that we love ourselves too much but rather that we overindulge the emotional content of our inner world. Every small trauma is intensified, intentionally; every small word our mother once said to us, every unimportant occasion of abandonment and disappointment. We are shocked to the core of our being, as if someone falsely promised us that life would be a tender place; as if we ourselves are so delicate that we must be always treated gently otherwise we might be smashed into pieces. And the question is what came first: have we truly been shaped so dramatically by all these traumas? Perhaps the very notion of being traumatized has equipped us with a justification for our condition and empowered our lack of responsibility. Is our hidden choice to remain a wounded child forever?

The simple fact is that we often adopt traumatic narratives that other people told us we still carry unconsciously, and not only from this lifetime but from other lifetimes.

We seem infinitely to need self-healing and self-acceptance, embracing our wounded self in so many ways. In New Age culture we shape our environments in the same manner: everybody is expected always to smile, to hug and to show uninterrupted kindness. Of course, in our alienated world this is not such a bad idea, but when we depend on these relaxing environments and healing atmospheres we become sensitive and vulnerable.

Anything that one might say to us is intensified in our inner lenses and might lead to a long period of self-wallowing and brooding. The process of self-observation - the emotional dynamics, the emotional examination and the self-study - sometimes seems more important than the actual result or action. This, along with the 'here and now' notion, nullifies all sense of directionality and moving forward. More than that, life itself in a way becomes a continuous shock, a form of subtle trauma.

Doesn't this unquenchable need for perpetual healing and self-acceptance hide within it a deeper sense of inadequacy and helplessness, bringing about a refusal to mature, to take responsibility, and to come out to a life that so frightens us? There is no question that being spiritual involves a high level of gentleness and capacity for self-observation, but when these qualities serve our deepest fear they transform into hypersensitivity, fragility and impotence.

I do not intend to discard the use of spiritual therapy or the essential purification process which may include the release of traumas. I merely point out that the centrality of these notions and practices in the New Age movement is destructive. We tend to forget that psychology is only a possible route, another way to view the human experience. In the ancient Yogic traditions hundreds of people attained liberation without having to go through the psychological path at all, so it is definitely not an essential spiritual work - purification of samskaras (deep-rooted memories) can be obtained through various means.

The claim that psychology is a necessity for the much more challenged Westerners is also invalid, since the art of facing life's pressures is demanding everywhere and at all times, in all conditions. The simple truth is that we are profoundly conditioned to see ourselves as psychological creatures, and this perception continuously enhances the psychological content and instills in it a complexity which doesn't exist objectively.

There are other views which may also be discovered as completely valid, such as collective cultural conditioning or (according to Viktor Frankl) spiritual neuroses and even made-up neuroses which are the result of the emptiness and boredom of our age.

Of course, there are trauma-stricken people in this world and others who genuinely require a psychological approach to their crises, and yet the *psychological world-view* must be put in its sane proportions. The general belief that in order to become transformed and liberated one must go through the release of traumas might reveal itself as just one more conditioning to let go. Psychology is indeed a new important layer in our growing complexity, but it is only a tool, not always the most efficient one, and certainly not a proper world-view.

We somehow tend to 'repress' here the spiritual-transformative view, which points profoundly at total liberation from the very psychological structure. We passionately hold on to some false image of a broken and wounded self, that will forever need to heal and look deeper and deeper into itself. Too often we neglect the earth-shaking spiritual insight that in our innermost there is really nothing to heal (or even to accept).

We don't realize the vicious circle, in which we ourselves keep creating the psychological self which we tirelessly observe and study; we nourish and maintain it by looking for traumatic origins, or by inventing them.

Infected by the psychological revolution, we over-personalize the inner world, forgetting that large portions of it are impersonal, and meaningless to poke at.

Spirituality is a new layer of consciousness, which surpasses the lower levels of sensation, emotion and thought. For this reason, it is bewildering to recognize the tremendous centrality of emotion in the New Age movement; what I 'feel' bears an amazing significance. After all, in the much broader context of the spiritual-transformative world-view, psychology is nothing but a frequency which, in an expanded state of consciousness, simply doesn't exist.

But the strange combination of the centrality of the subjective and the psychological, along with the basic feeling of inadequacy, have eventually developed into an escapist narcissism which is unable to consider the ending of the psychological stream. Thus the true self has turned into a psychological preference of the subjective and the personal view and a general reluctance towards all externals.

If we ever want to be free, collectively, from this stranglehold of the psychological world-view, we must first and foremost face our deepest fear which makes us hold onto the hypersensitive self. Instead of escaping life, we must build our three lower chakras with the clear intention to finally come out, to be seen in this world and to partake in it as fully engaged co-creators. We must destroy the vulnerability - not the gentleness! - and cultivate the strength and power which simply couldn't emerge in the atmosphere of psychological fragility.

We must also realize that psychology is meant to enable a quickening of our liberation process, and if it doesn't, the reason is that we got trapped in it because *we wanted to be trapped*, motivated by a hidden obsession to somehow be rescued from the life in the world.

Chapter Five:

The Death of the Guru

*Celebrating the death of the external God and the death of the divine authority, the Guru, we forgot that individuality has its price! * Read about the real implications of self-authority and self-responsibility.*

> "... In this there is no teacher, no pupil; there is no leader; there is no guru; there is no Master, no Savior. You yourself are the teacher and the pupil; you are the Master; you are the guru; you are the leader; you are everything".
>
> [Jiddu Krishnamurti, spiritual teacher and philosopher]

Alongside the psychological revolution, and in some respects inseparable from it, there came forth the revolution of individuality. Arising from the ashes of the burnt-out 'isms' (the absolute collective truths), the individual used the springboard of the human rights revolution in order to take a leap into a world in which its center of gravity was subjective experience. Everything in the 20th century supported this step. Before anything else, it was the crumbling of religion's dominion and the death of the mythological God, enabled by cutting-edge philosophy, psychology, biology, physics and cosmology, which nourished the increasing power of the individual self.

Slowly but surely a new entity gathered forces to emerge as the new center of reality: a sovereign and autonomous self, which directs its 'own life' by its own power.

After thousands of years of human culture, in which religion or politics or great cultural and social movements controlled and directed the life of the human, all at once the individual gained his own life, which implied not only the basic freedom of opinion and speech, but also on a deeper level, that being unburdened by authority he was actually free to *choose* for himself what he wished to consume as 'reality' and what he wished to reject as 'non-reality'. This meant that the individual was now the one to determine and maintain his own connection (or disconnection) with the higher, more sublime reality - and the first establishment that was shaken to the root in this context was the proud line of spiritual and religious mediators that stood between the human and the alleged God.

In this atmosphere - in which rabbis and priests and others of this kind were being mashed by the urge of individuation - the Guru institute couldn't have survived either its transference into the West. Although the Western 20th century greeted curiously and courteously the many Eastern Gurus who appeared from the East and consequently gave birth to Eastern-inspired Western Gurus, the fundamental notion of the Guru as a divine and unquestionable authority, a notion which did so well in the East, could have never taken deep roots in our restless land.

There were at least a few reasons for the irrelevance of the Guru principle to the Western culture. The first major reason which I have already mentioned was the profound philosophical venture that had started at the end of the 19th century, best symbolized by Darwin, which gradually made it impossible for the great religions to maintain their dominion over the human mind.

Religion as a world-view was mortally wounded by the new emerging world-view which celebrated the death of the external God. This did not end with the father-like figure of God - it actually shook to the core the very notion of the patriarchal father. Humanity lost any kind of external father and, for good or bad, became an orphan. This included inevitably the father's authoritative representatives upon this earth, be it a rabbi, a priest or a Guru.

To this philosophical and scientific shake-up we must add the crumbling of all other 'isms' taking place due to humanity's disillusionment with absolutist collective ideas. Needless to say, the peak was World War II which seemed like a dreadful experiment derived from a collective trance caused by pathologically insane utopian ideas. Reluctance towards any charismatic authority and collective societal mania that has solidified within us ever since the endless chain of disasters in the first part of the 20th century, has made it impossible for us to blindly give in to some higher power entitled to take away our free will and choice. Indeed, the emphasis in the democratic West on inner and outer freedom, the sanctification of free choice and self-fulfillment and of course the increased strength of the human rights movement, has turned the mystical demand for unconditional surrender and devotion to the Guru impossible. This may seem alluring to a few of us, but generally it is irrelevant and even grotesque in a Western context.

Generally it seems that the Guru principle contradicts the foundation of the Western spirit. Most characterized by its restless and wakeful inquiry, rational and logical mind and suspicious doubting which tends to destabilize any kind of over-satisfied paradigm, this spirit just doesn't seem to be one which is capable of embracing the mystified notion of the Guru.

Naturally, the moment Eastern teachings entered the West they found it hard to enforce their highly patterned structures on the Western mind. Instead, everything here in our New Age movement finds eclectic souls who are always keen on new possibilities, yet are not submissive by nature and maintain freedom of choice, while on the verge of decadent consumerism.

Another important reason for the irrelevance of the Guru principle nowadays is the many scandals which overshadowed the activity of so many Eastern and Western Gurus. In the West there are no holy cows, and there was very little room for blind justification of all the alleged claims regarding Gurus' patterns of behavior.

The many contradictions (or apparent contradictions) found in the teachings and personalities of spiritual teachers have shattered the romantic and idealist perception of the Guru as God's perfect extension. Of course, there may be a chance that conclusions have been made too hurriedly and clumsily, yet it seems justified for the West to bear little patience in regard to the frozen images of the Guru principle.

Some important 20th century teachers have even encouraged the passing away of spiritual authority. Osho passionately promoted the destruction of religious authority, and

Krishnamurti trod even further on this pathway, calling for a total negation of the Guru institute. Many others, who didn't go that far, still supported this step by emphasizing incessantly the 'God is within you' notion, and by instilling the idea that there is no separation whatsoever between the self and the source of life, weakened dramatically the roll of the mediating authority.

The death of the Guru principle doesn't imply a total irrelevance of *spiritual expertise*. On the contrary, it strips off the unnecessary mythology and superstition and leaves us with the naked truth: that a spiritual master is nothing more than an expert on spiritual transformation, and that just like any other expert - be it a medical doctor or an artist - we consult with him as long as his field of expertise is needed in our life.

Abandoning any kind of idealization, which liberates us from quite insane expectations, one would go to a spiritual master in the same way one is being qualified for a certain field of learning in College or University. As we so naturally expect from experts in our life, the spiritual master also must submit himself to ethical restrictions: no personal involvement in the student's life; no control and no enforcement of one's will, out of the profound recognition that a genuine respect for one's free will is the only solid foundation of individual evolution. Perhaps one day the West will institutionalize spiritual training in a more academic context and thus free us all from this all too familiar and confusing diffusion.

The rise of the individual, along with the fall of the religious and spiritual authority, has brought about a tremendous freedom. The thing we missed here is the fact that *along with freedom comes responsibility*. The moment one gains sovereignty he also becomes fully in charge of oneself: he is solely responsible to liberate himself from all suffering; he is the one who must lay out his entire spiritual journey; he has to enforce on himself structures and laws which he alone defines, and he alone pours meaning and purpose into the empty vessel of his own transformation. Evolutionarily speaking, this is a great leap, since it endorses the gradual gravitation towards an internal spirituality and thus strengthens the idea of 'No power outside of man'.

The individual and the divine become truly one and the same. The only question is, are we ready to take this leap? And the poor answer is: wait, not yet!

Celebrating the freedom of the fatherless child who no longer needs to obey any external rule, can be fun for a while, yet we must understand that psychologically becoming fatherless is both a terrifying and powerful predicament; it holds within it a tremendous potential, and with it the possibility of self-destruction.

Having no one and nothing to lean upon means that we must deeply uproot within ourselves the hidden psychological need for a father-figure, and then face the possible spiritual ramifications and implications.

We have neglected our duty to face the state of 'no external God and therefore no external Guru'. Death of the father-figure, and with it the end of divine spiritual authority, implies that there is truly no external directing and organizing force, and if we want to pursue the trail of genuine individuality we should understand that at its other end awaits us nothing but the realization that it all depends on us.

Individuality comes at a price: combined with authentic spirituality, it means that we cannot rely on anything, cannot wait or hope for anything, because there's nobody out there - if anyone should know the directions of the journey, this is us and only us. This is the problem with freedom of choice; it is wonderful, yet deeply confusing. It leaves us and us alone with the responsibility to fill the void of our own self-creation.

Perhaps if we have seriously understood the true implication of self-authority, we would have immediately regretted the death of the father. By shattering the mythologically divine father we are left with only one route which our free choice allows us; either to avoid it and get stuck forever, or boldly step into it. We have to grow up towards a wholesome responsibility; the son must become the father.

For that, the Western spiritual individual of our times must gather forces and imbue his journey with new conscious qualities. He must learn how to walk alone against the stream of the world, since he doesn't belong anymore to great protective collectives; he, as individual, must face by himself the forces of the world and maintain his own spiritual power and authority.

Being alone, he must cultivate his own renunciation, overcoming by his own power all temptations, addictions and comforts which are offered abundantly in the too convenient Western world. In absence of the stabilizing and protective spiritual environment, it is hard to overcome oneself and develop profound self-discipline. One has to fortify his own journey, since he cannot hide in a cave or monastery.

This is a tremendous responsibility for our own transformation. We must work hard and tirelessly strive in order to create the sufficient self-effort required for this evolutionary leap. Where there's no self-effort, self-authority is impossible. The individual has merely gained the undesirable 'freedom' to give himself excuses, to avoid and to give up, to loosen self-discipline and choose convenience whenever things become too 'hard' and too 'demanding'.

In traditions and under the guidance of powerful authorities we were given the way, perpetually empowered by other external forces to hold on to our effort and to never let go.

But since by its very nature our Western spirituality develops precisely in the absence of structures and frameworks, we are left unsupported; fully independent but also without context and direction. How easily we sink and let go!

Our major problem is that having no external structures, we can hardly maintain even the most extraordinary explosions of awakening. This calls for a new ability to create for ourselves structures of meaning and purpose. This does not mean that we shouldn't use the signposts of knowledge bestowed on us by spiritual experts - only that signposts can't really develop within us the capacity to choose and to respond in the midst of our stormy daily life.

We are obliged to gather enough forces from within in order to liberate ourselves from suffering (being the ones who have created it in the first place), and to cultivate an independent, wakeful intelligence that can define its own values and context in a relativistic world.

After all, even absolute and external morality cannot save us; instead, we ought to replace morality with listening moment to moment, defining what is right and what is wrong with every step, and thus embracing both freedoms and burdens that lie in being real individuals.

Chapter Six:

A Pre-modern Ghost

*Read about the effect of the remnants of the great religions on the New Age movement * How we mixed transformation with superstition, belief and hope, and got seriously stuck with a pre-modern ghost.*

> "The further the spiritual evolution of mankind advances, the more certain it seems to me that the path to genuine religiosity does not lie through the fear of life, and the fear of death, and blind faith, but through striving after rational knowledge".
>
> [Albert Einstein, scientist]

Generally speaking, there are two kinds of spirituality: transformative spirituality and comforting spirituality.

The comforting spirituality is designed to provide its believer with mental, emotional and practical tools in order to handle the challenge of life. These tools, a reservoir of concepts or thought-forms which are supposedly derived from some superior truth, enable the believer to mask and filter the harsh and direct experience of life by imagining that it is all somehow ruled by a cosmic logic, a divine providence, a hidden order that encompasses our world and even silently monitors it. For this reason, comforting spirituality can be also defined as 'conceptualized spirituality'. This connection to divine order bestows on the believer a sense of calm and comfort. Bosomed by this perfect sense and linked to a higher power that surpasses all visible realities, he is also being filled with a bogus sense of power and the patronization or subtle revenge that lie in the illusion of overpowering forces which in the visible world are much stronger than him.

In contrast to comforting spirituality, transformative spirituality does not aim at providing tools for self-defense, since it is not interested in masking and filtering life's direct experience. On the contrary, it shatters all comforting concepts and strives to nullify the 'self' which maintains the duality with life, and which is essentially already made up of more or less sophisticated protective mechanisms.

The comforting spirituality is very typical of religions' teachings for the masses, from Christianity to Tibetan Buddhism - it is, so to say, 'opium for the masses' - while transformative spirituality has been forever concealed within small core-groups at the heart of the great Western religions and in more extensive frameworks in the Eastern religions. Too often the two kinds of spirituality have been inseparably interwoven - even great Gurus were seen serving offerings to Shiva!

One can also think of comforting spirituality as the remnants of pre-modern thinking; based upon ancient and unproved beliefs and totally outdated cosmological contexts, it has survived the logical and rational renaissance by feeding on our deepest fears and needs for security and order. And this pre-modern thinking is still dripping its influence on us through the remaining power of ancient religions over the primitive layers of our minds. However, in our New Age movement we haven't managed to discern these antique influences, partly because this need for external logic and order suits perfectly our hidden fear of the cruel and whimsical life. Another reason seems to be the fact that pre-modern thinking appears magical, colorful and enticing - one can rejoice in having so much to hold on to, there is always beside us a calming duality and with it many thought-forms to keep us company. Transformative spirituality in comparison seems so dreadfully alone and naked!

Yet, if we want to evolve as a movement, one of the most important steps we can ever take is to clearly distinguish between these two kinds of spirituality, and then to consciously and proudly shake off the comforting spirituality and choose the transformative kind - a direct and naked spirituality, which is not based on beliefs and hopes, and which does not lean on some false future of another promised world or time. One must keep in mind that the ability to survive thousands of years of evolution does not necessarily imply truthfulness - on the contrary, our role now is to extract only the direct transformative essence of religions and to discard all the rest.

So what are the essential components of comforting spirituality? Clearly, the most fundamental principle is that *we are not alone*. Something - be it the higher power of the mythological God, protective entities such as angels and fairies and even superior aliens, channeled forces or sacred symbols and sites - is comfortingly out there, protecting and guiding us and constantly pouring the sweetness of order and logic into this violent evolutionary madhouse. Indeed, since the dawn of time God and his spirits have faithfully served us, humans, as the unseen complementary of all the meaningless and unexplained events of the phenomenal world.

Of course, in order to actually 'experience' that we're not alone, we first have to take on ourselves the belief that we're not alone, since any force outside of the visible universe entails believing. Consequently, this belief, put as a presupposition, allows us to confirm and re-confirm the 'existence' of such things through mental projections and dubious reinforcements from external reality.

The second fundamental is *hope*. As we so fervently believe, and as we already 'know' that there exists an underlying order behind the chaos, the next most 'logical' conclusion is that this divine principle, being responsible for conducting it all, can quite easily grant us at will whatever it is we wish for. On the ground of hope prayer naturally flourishes and the constant, distant gaze towards a 'better future' enkindles the believer's heart.

Hope skillfully weaves the mythology which reinforces the possibility of gratification in this world or in the afterlife (a much improved version of living). Miracles, the undoubtable verifications of God's intervention in the world, burst out at every corner, and when they fail to relieve our pain, there are always other dimensions, such as the kingdom of heaven or the world to come, and there are always other times, such as the end times or judgment day, or even other states such as the next (and better) incarnation. This equips us with a superior logic for the human drama:

though this is unclear in the visible world, one can be assured that behaving righteously now will credit him in another time or space; the saintly person will be greatly rewarded while all the nasty, indulgent people of the present world will be scorned.

In our New Age movement the great anticipation for the 2012 shift which has enticed so many is a good example of the way religious pre-modern hope takes more sophisticated, seemingly trans-rational forms. The messiah and redemption are by no means different from the 2012 mania or any other earth-shaking sacred dates.

Consolation is yet another fundamental. The perfect hidden order of the world also provides us with mental pain relievers for the time being. Whenever we encounter painful events, we can immediately calm ourselves through concepts such as 'all is God's will', 'everything is for the best', 'this is God's test' and 'God has given and God has taken away'. Facing hard and demanding upheavals, we hurriedly look for a great hidden purpose and an intentional directing will of some divine scheme. We can even go so far as to embrace a totally deterministic approach, in which one is choiceless, bound to act and to react according to some well-designed plan.

Mixing hope and consolation also brings about a sense of *illusory power*. We may relish the idea of the imagined power awaiting us in the 'other world' or take comfort in the thought that our 'profit', though non-material, increasingly grows. But we can also intoxicate ourselves by feeling that our hopes and intentions can dramatically influence the visible reality of the present world. This gives rise to many disguised pre-modern thoughts in our post-modern minds: positive thoughts, the law of attraction, self-healing from *any* kind of disease (since every disease is supposedly the result of our thinking!), and so on.

The last fundamental of comforting spirituality is *morality*. Morality is a given set of behavioral codes, that by following it we are being credited by some higher power and higher order as being 'virtuous' enough to take our seat beside the angels. We become 'holy' and 'saintly' if we only make sure that we are pure enough. Purity here implies disliking this material world enough to turn our backs on all lower urges of the flesh. It means aspiring towards some form of apathy to the world of time and space, as we are divinely-originated spiritual beings, who only briefly visit the earth. This celestial notion of the 'never-really-born' soul also links our minds with a higher, external order. Again, if we keep upgrading our self by means of constant effort to correct our thoughts, behavior and deeds, 'one day' we might reach our destination - either be perfected or get rewarded in some way (returning to the Nirvanic source or enjoying the pleasures of heaven).

Our Western spirituality must shake off all traces of comforting spirituality, as this spirituality thrives on pre-modern mythologies. Before anything else, it must rid itself of the very principle of belief. Belief has nothing to do with the spiritual transformation of a sober Western mind.

There may or may not be external and higher directing forces - no one really knows. So why should it be included in our transformative equations? How can it support our evolution? Obviously it cannot; on the contrary, it terribly weakens us on this inner venture. The grace of the Lord, the healing angels, the blue Shiva, the superior alien - who needs them and what for? Is it because we're afraid of remaining truly alone in this endless and empty universe? And if that is the case, shouldn't we face this fear and accept our (possibly temporary) aloneness?

The dualistic feeling, maintained by pre-modern belief, keeps us away from authentic Western spirituality, which cannot include external forces that require faith. Unfortunately, we are heavily burdened with superstition regarding unproven entities which allegedly surround us. Though magical and colorful, this may be nothing but a lonely child's wishful thinking. At any rate, a movement which is inspired by great teachers and philosophers who are perfectly capable of grasping the mysteries of the universe by themselves, does not need external forces and channelers who bring out some otherworldly help.

God, understood as the totality of existence, is no longer a directing force but an essence to unite with. This is a great paradigm shift, and understandably we haven't managed yet to erase all fingerprints of pre-modern thinking. There may be no external meaning to existence, and even if there is some directing intelligence, it may have left it totally open for us to consciously instill meaning and direction. Darwin, modern cosmology and philosophy have already efficiently demonstrated an evolution that works itself out, leveling its direction from within.

From this angle, hope can be viewed as a typical expression of the pre-modern split between matter and spirit. Not really wanting to be here makes us mentally wander to some alternative space and time, be it the improved humanity of 2012 or the kingdom of heaven or even a better incarnation. Furthermore, prayer, religious rituals and worship, which preserve the outdated personalized Gods, may be of no relevance, as there's no one to pray to and no grace to anxiously wait for.

Consolation through the power of concepts is self-deceit. Concepts must be realized as nothing but pain-relievers which cure nothing; a way to find some 'inner' gain and purpose to suffering in order to avoid the purity of pain. After all, truth is not to be found in concepts but rather in liberating ourselves from all concepts. For example, the notion of the 'will of God' can breathe its last now.

The theological habit that there is a divine intention behind wars and diseases means nothing today. We used to explain dying of pneumonia or being born too hairy as 'God's will', but now we can see that what seemed to be a divine subjugation becomes, through science, easily solved. There is also no divine will behind terrible wars - only lower levels of human development, which make people capable of doing such things. Human evolution is a sufficient explanation that shakes off all external reasons and intentions.

The very opposite of the deterministic 'God's will' - the much-exaggerated credit for reality-altering thought and intention - seems, in this context, like a form of post-modern witchcraft. And also tracing 'messages from the spirit' through coincidental events. Here, again, we want to feel that the universe is meaningful and filled with external directions, but these may be nothing but mental projections, driven by a zealous need to gain power and control over a totally random universe (as established, at least partially, through quantum physics).

Lastly, morality, part and parcel of comforting spirituality, is the distorted perception of the nature of purity, a perception which is derived from the split between spirit and matter. Instead of a saintliness which prefers the abstract over the material, a new state of wakeful listening will reveal to the Western mind an inner morality that unfolds moment to moment and that can swiftly change to adjust to new evolutionary needs. Eternally improving ourselves in order to attain perfection or reward may just as well be realized as an old religious habit, based on sin, guilt and fake humility. Transformative spirituality, on the other hand, is the quantum leap of consciousness which can bring about transformation beyond time, process and perpetual improvement.

An authentic Western spirituality, being committed to the basic sanity of evolved Western logic, will negate the superstitions of belief, the same way we have gotten rid of many other superstitions such as the warning that masturbation might be dangerous. It will realize comforting concepts as lesser forms of spirituality, and will extract from religions their very essence: the religious spirit. This kind of spirit stands alone in the midst of the universe, without prayer, hope, consolation and morality. Awed by the internal sacredness of the cosmos, it will silently face the fathomless mystery of being and becoming and will be filled by it, not expecting for a single moment to be saved by divine order or external meaning. Then it will merge unconditionally into the totality of the universe itself.

Chapter Seven:

The Call

Read how fear has kept us hiding in the periphery of the Western life, while our greatest call is to move into the center and help change our world

> "Many people meditate in order that a third eye may open. For that they feel they should close their two physical eyes. They thereby become blind to the world. But the fact is that the third eye will never open. We can never close our eyes to the world in the name of spirituality. Self-realization is the ability to see ourselves in all beings. This is the third eye through which you see, even while your two eyes are open"
>
> [Mata Amritanandamayi, spiritual teacher]

Recently, a friend of mine took part in some intense one-day spiritual gathering. After the thorough contemplation and meditation had come to an end, while the room was imbued with the fragrance of spiritual heights, she asked the other participants: "Don't you feel that it does not suffice to immerse in these good-feeling states - shouldn't we somehow pour it towards troubled people, such as the hungry refugees in our country?"

They all gazed at her, perplexed, and then responded: "How could you be so conceptual after this wonderful workshop?"

How have we reached such an awkward predicament, in which an overflowing spiritual heart is considered to be 'conceptual'? How come cramming ourselves endlessly with spiritual feel-good experiences doesn't ever lead to the broken heartedness and active engagement which are the direct, organic result of higher awareness? Isn't it the natural course of things that in breaking through all limitations of individuality one would feel immensely responsible for the greater whole?

Yes, it is natural that having no distinctive barriers between the world at large and yourself would leave you extraordinarily vulnerable to the state of the world, and yet even in these explosions of unity we, in the New Age movement, are unconsciously left protected because of the deadly combination of our collective narcissistic epidemic - an essential side effect of post-modern individualism - and, more esoterically speaking, our three unbalanced lower chakras.

Our movement is astoundingly feeble and passive, apathetically watching the stream of the world like an outside spectator. We are like the too-vulnerable and nearly autistic child who blankly gazes at the window, playing with imaginary things while the rest of his class is fully engrossed in learning and socializing.

The whole world swirls in a tremendously creative enterprise, while our aloof movement dwells somewhere in the periphery of the Western life. Of course, it stands on a completely unstable ground, due to the loose connections with both Eastern and Western philosophical lineages, but this is not the primary reason.

As I have already pointed earlier in this book, the most deep-rooted source of this apathy is that the very motivation that drives this movement is evading life's greatest call.

Supported by the already narcissistic design of pre-modern individualism, our movement stands on the shaky ground of three unbalanced lower chakras. As long as one's three lower chakras are not forged by the bold fires of true transformation, as long as we overlook the challenge of these three lower chakras, we essentially lack fundamental love of life, engaged passion and strong enough self to withstand any pressure or demand. This inevitably leads to unwillingness to actually be here, the result of which is the gradual formation of sophisticated means of escape. Though this escape frequently masquerades as liberation from the world, there is a stark difference between genuine spiritual maturation which outgrows the world, and contracting and withdrawing from life; it only *sounds* the same.

One common way of escape, discussed at length in the sixth chapter of this manifesto, is developing comforting concepts and superstitions. Thriving on conceptual spirituality and regressive wishful thinking, we imagine ourselves as not really belonging to this world but rather linked with some other space or time. A second way, discussed in the fourth chapter, is psychological wallowing: turning the most selfless activity in this world - spiritual development - into the most narcissistic, self-engrossed activity.

In this over-personalized context, everything sinks into a self-reflective obsession. Even helping the world would be but a reflection of my own inner process and would serve solely for that purpose. As I pointed out earlier, narcissism is self-generated and endlessly creates countless new neuroses, which in turn require their own 'healing' process.

Moreover, there is the tendentious inclination towards the female aspects of Eastern spirituality, while overlooking the great emphasis on conscious effort and self-overcoming. As discussed in the second chapter, surrender and acceptance have become efficient forms of avoidance. By indulging ourselves in the overly relaxed 'nothing to do and nowhere to go' notion, we have managed to shirk the depths of spiritual responsibility.

Beyond that, there is always a well-concealed wish to renounce the world and retire to some monastic form of living. This is, of course, a devious way to fool ourselves, since we're not truly ready to become genuine renunciates - we still like to enjoy Western middle class comfort. This is only a way to live between two worlds, excelling in neither and keep on daydreaming.

Remaining divorced from reality, living in the distant outskirts of society, we resist growth, as growing up (so we unconsciously recognize) implies new responsibility; after all, to be spiritually awake means to take on the entire weight of the world on one's shoulders. But who wants that, when one dislikes life and would prefer to roam in other, more idealistic dimensions?

This fearful disregard for life can never be demolished unless we learn to stand on our firm three lower chakras through purposeful spiritual therapy, broader context and serious spiritual depth. The catch, of course, is the fact that an inseparable part of the unbalanced three lower chakras is the unwillingness to face this challenge in the first place.

As soon as our three lower chakras are stabilized, we will be all at once capable of consciously choosing to partake in the tremendous creative undertaking of the Western spirit. We will be able to discover that there is nothing more awkward for us than remaining in the periphery of the Western world, especially given the fact that we possess an astounding potential contribution; in fact, we are somehow destined to hand some of the most crucial keys for the further evolution of mankind.

The basic truth of spiritual transformation will be obvious to us then: the only tangible indication of the mystical breakthrough of self-barriers is a passionate devotion to the whole; an extreme vulnerability to life's needs which nullifies the narcissistic vulnerability to our own emotional stream.

Then, and only then, could we consider the nature of the Western spirit and its corresponding spirituality. After all, as already discussed in chapter three, we don't possess yet a spirituality of our own. Western spirituality has been positioned against the Western spirit, as if it was its perfect antithesis: 'doing' has been overpowered by 'non-doing', 'becoming' has been replaced with 'immovability' and so on, and with a great deal of commercial hype this has been somehow established as the essential nature of spirituality itself.

Thus we should question the very foundations of spirituality, and by doing so make conscious our Western inclination and fate. Daringly, we should search within the interior of the Western spirit to reveal its true nature, and then upgrade our spirituality accordingly, reorienting it to our real mental environment - the 21st century Western society.

So what are really the outlines of the Western spirit? It is easy to notice that the West is more extroverted and inclined towards objectivism in contrast to the more introverted and subjective East. The West puts much emphasis on the senses and the phenomenal world; through technology (constant improvement of life) and science (the objective search for truth), and through its evolutionary leaning. The West is ceaseless movement, becoming and changing, while the East is more withdrawing and immovable. It was not a coincidence that the famous Western proverb 'Don't just sit there - do something!' has been mischievously distorted by Indian Guru Osho into the book title 'Don't just do something - be there!'

Put crudely, two forms of coping with life are offered to us in the spiritual arena: the first is the Eastern-oriented simplified approach, which as the name suggests propels us towards a total simplification of life, concentrating the entire complexity into one focal point of being that ideally 'solves it all'; the second is the Western-oriented complex world-view that offers a careful observation of all the different dimensions of life along with an honest dealing with them - of course, *out of* the one-pointed being.

In spite of the growing interest in enlightened teachings, it seems like there is a justified anticipation in today's world that these teachings will espouse the second approach, which equips us with direct and explicit answers to the biggest question of them all: "How can one make it through the amazingly complex Western life?"

The thing is that fundamentally, there shouldn't be any difference between being truly liberated in all possible layers of one's being and finding a perfect and wholesome response to all of life's challenges.

Essentially, enlightenment *is* the full knowledge of coping with all of life's challenges, so liberation equals the perfect response to the challenge of Western life. Thus, all separation can finally be abolished and liberation, otherworldly only in its outdated interpretation, may reveal itself as the ultimate answer to the challenge presented to us by postmodern life.

The pre-modern religions of the West are more inclined towards dualism - relationship between God and the soul - while non-duality, the unification of one's consciousness with the all-inclusive reality, is much more prominent in Eastern religions. This is also important to note that while Eastern spirituality is often characterized by the 'eternal smile', the history of Western religions contains much more frustration, anger, rebellion and the effort to influence politics and social structures (think for a moment of Moses, Jesus and Mohammed in contrast to Buddha, Confucius, Lao Tzu and Adi Shankara). In the East, there is a somewhat deterministic position in regard to the external flow of events, while the West has quite persistently demonstrated an anti-deterministic stand, forever emphasizing choice and will.

It is intriguing to note that Nietzsche mocked the Buddha for his claim that one should abolish any will to life and thus be released into Nirvana. Nietzsche's observation is that it is actually a self-deception to think one can truly abolish will, since will to power is the driving force of all life. Thus, one can only sublimate the will to power by turning it inwardly, towards Nirvana.

The Buddha, in this light, did not let go of will but rather turned his will towards the nothingness (wanting nothingness instead of wanting life). From a Western world-view this is not only a sound argument but also one which finally provides us with a deeper legitimacy for the 'will' which Eastern spiritually has so hurriedly negated.

Attempting to let go of will in the West seems like a terribly contradictory, highly counterproductive effort, while integrating will into our new spirituality may be realized as one of the most essential stepping-stones for a logically coherent philosophy of transformation. Adding to that Nietzsche's conviction that without friction there cannot be evolution - a negation of the Eastern striving towards homeostasis - we may begin to consider the beginning of a spirituality that springs from power rather than from weakness.

In general, the Eastern spirit does not lean towards the notions of directionality, final purpose or destination. The sense of time is mostly cyclical, and if at all, the final destination is to escape the purposeless stream of change in order to evaporate into the pure spirit. This, of course, has given rise to the corresponding atmosphere of our New Age movement, in which there is no goal or direction, since the process itself is the goal; the perception of time as evolution crumbles into the absolutism of the 'here and now', sucking every possible future into an oblivious and relaxed nothing.

Since 'whatever comes up in the moment' and the unending process of learning become a purpose unto itself, the very sense of moving forward is obliterated. But in the West, which is imbued with the feeling (and knowledge) of evolution, it makes no sense to have no direction, purpose or meaningful 'omega point'.

While the context of the Eastern spirit is generally personal and subjective (redeeming the soul from the cycle of birth and death), the Western spirit takes delight in observing all processes from an objective outlook, scientifically perceiving even the most internal process as a mere expression of a much more general process.

Endowing the subjective reality with a status of 'Truth absolute' is thus not consistent with our fundamental design. For example, the 'all is well' of Eastern spirit seems awkward for a tremendously activist and engaged spirit - how can it be that 'all is well' while clearly all is not well?

For the true Western spirit, a spirituality that feeds on the 'all is well' notion is a dead spirituality. A genuine Western spirituality bears a social role; it has its active part in the scheme of the world, and it cannot turn its back on society, murmuring 'all is well'. What seems beautiful in the context of Eastern spirituality might seem in the context of the Western spirit as narcissism: thriving on the notion of individual redemption while the house is on fire!

Taking no part in the creative enterprise of our world - and even worse, taking pride in having no part in it - is the very opposite of the Western spirit. Ignoring the fact that even the 'personal' act of expanding our consciousness takes place for the sake of the evolution of our species; forgetting that we're nullifying the personal self only so we can serve the world, are the new forms of 'ignorance' of reality and truth. Hence, awakening new motivation and context for our spiritual development - turning our 'personal' evolution into a conscious contribution - is one essential step on the way towards Western spirituality.

Chapter Eight:

A Stand in the World

Read more about our greatest call to move into the center and help change our world.

> "All the world's major religions, with their emphasis on love, compassion, patience, tolerance, and forgiveness can and do promote inner values. But the reality of the world today is that grounding ethics in religion is no longer adequate. This is why I am increasingly convinced that the time has come to find a way of thinking about spirituality and ethics beyond religion altogether".
>
> [The 14th Dalai Lama, spiritual teacher and Tibetan leader]

Unity consciousness in the West does not express itself naturally as a total withdrawal into some sublime and subjective state of consciousness. For us, to be united implies that we are all one complex of matter and spirit, evolving and rising towards new heights that can further transform our manifest world. This should not be understood as a mere abstraction: it means an actual engagement in the process, gathering our forces of developing awareness for the sake of a process which is much greater than ourselves. It is true that 'there's nowhere to go' - but only in the sense that fantasizing about a transcendental escape means nothing to us as we are too engrossed in the present magnificent process of becoming; a becoming that is sacred in itself, since it is the very extension of divine will.

The New Age movement should be viewed from this angle as a *social reform movement*. From the ashes of the fearful and selfish scattered New Age community a conscious intention should arise - to develop and hand down the keys for a world-change. This new movement must work from within the world; aided by the depth of its wholesome, uninterrupted consciousness it will realize that really nothing is well.

Its most essential wisdom, the conviction that the qualities of a transcendental mind can revolutionize the world of time and space, should be demonstrated in thousands of ways until the time comes and the human society recognizes that it cannot go any further without the transformed spirit.

It is time for us to abandon our dens, get used to the scorching sunlight and be seen in this world. While the revolution of the sixties was heavily infected by childish enthusiasm, and was more an outburst than a true revolution, at least the 'flower children' were endowed with an energetic surge that we so acutely lack now. By evoking our suppressed Western powers - ambitious effort, restless activism, evolutionary tension, intellectual discrimination and will to influence - we can start right away, not brooding and waiting for the 'right action' to somehow appear but simply begin and let direct experience shape our way.

So apart from a profound inner purification and transformation - done in the clear context of our newfound environmental responsibility - it is also time for us to take a stand in the world: to herald our claim while agreeing to 'get our hands dirty' in the process of engagement. In this kind of world, not taking a stand, remaining a proud or just apathetic onlooker, is in many respects immoral. Indeed, being so fearful of the painful demands of this world, it is but natural for us to only want to feel good, and this is why we so readily embrace misconceived notions such as 'all is good just as it is' as our reference point to life itself while this is really only true as a background meditative cognition. And yet, it is very liberating to realize that whatever it is that makes us feel good can also stealthily keep us in bondage.

We will be amazed to realize how narcissism and all of its diseased by-products dissolve all at once the moment we gain the exciting sense of belonging to the world and playing a valuable and most needed part in its scheme. So many 'psychological patterns' that have been troubling us for decades, and that seemed to be demanding tremendous processes of analysis and healing, will simply evaporate in the quicker vibration of higher destiny.

Then we will understand, not intellectually but rather directly, that large parts of our psychological perception of ourselves have been self-created and are not even important to untie or to heal. Herein lies a great secret: by rising above the merely personal to live in a way that benefits humanity, we don't only establish a new moral foundation for our lives, but we elevate ourselves to a level in which most of our psychological contractions naturally wither away.

We have become self-obsessed *because* of an acute lack of meaning and direction. We have been misled to believing that spirituality is all about 'going within' (and hopefully never coming back), but the moment we grasp our substantial Dharma it will be clear that knowing our role can immediately detach us from an entire illusory world that has kept us occupied for so long, imagining that we 'must sort ourselves out before we are truly ready to help the world'.

Indeed, our New Age movement is entrapped in its self-created world which goes nowhere. It only spins in its own circular maze. By simply moving from this healing session to that new meditation technique we hold ourselves captive within a closed circle of self-improvement that effectively leads to no breakthrough as it has no other end; this may go as far as speaking of our eventual 'coming out to the world' as if we were kept in incubators. Even then, what immediately follows is the unconsciously frightened thought: "In that case, now I *really* need more therapy and meditation otherwise how can I clear all the blockages that make it impossible for me to come out to the world!"

Perhaps the most transformative solution is a total upside down solution: we are increasingly freer the more we lose interest in our imaginary selves - and even when there are genuinely conflicting patterns, we can clear them 'on the way', not as part of a journey that has its own internal, personalized purpose but so we can make ourselves even more available.

Yes, we are desperately needed in this world, and any one of us should fathom his own contribution, be it seeding the Western society with ideas or social service and activism. By simply moving from the shady background to the illuminated front stage, we will comprehend just how essential we are. We are destined to act at the center of things, to guide human evolution and to translate our profound knowledge into incredible and revolutionary tools. Although there are numerous social reform movements in the world, our uniqueness lies in the knowledge of consciousness and the transformative ripples it can emit towards the visible world.

However, these words of encouragement should not be interpreted as a new, sophisticated way in which our fear of the world takes the form of yet another twisted spiritual pride. The more one knows his responsibility, the humbler one becomes, for there is forever so much to do and whatever it is that we manage to fulfill will always be but a tiny fraction of the potential contribution. Thus we *partake* in the flow of the world and become an integral part of it, rather than hovering over it as if from the heights of some illusory spiritual dimensions.

In my eyes, the most important stride we could ever take in our attempt at stepping into the evolutionary stream is to actually form a united movement out of the dispersed schools and streams. This kind of movement will have to thoughtfully consider the foundations and implications of an authentic Western spirituality, that can truly help change the world.

A genuine New Age movement will unveil and then uproot the fear that runs beneath our spirituality and, recognizing the cultural framework in which it grows, will boldly choose the Western world. This movement will ask - of course, in many diverse and often contradictory voices - 'Why are we here? Is it a mere coincidence or is there a different meaning to belonging to the Western heritage?'

This movement may go as far as understanding that we only should extricate the essentials of the Eastern spirit, but really forge our own independent spirituality, which is completely entwined around the Western spirit. Recognizing that the West presents its unique challenges that inevitably give shape to a different kind of spirituality, it will consolidate an evolving, caring and fully engaged spiritual way of being, which wholeheartedly embraces the becoming, ever-unfolding universe.

A Western spiritual movement will give birth to a new impulse of caring which directly stems from the union of emptiness and fullness. It will passionately shatter the thin line that has separated the objective, material life and the subjective, eternal spirit. It will bring forth an open-eyed spirituality, that doesn't close its eyes in order to see God but rather keeps them both wide open. While the revelation of the true self has led the Eastern mind towards absorption, here it will rise as a new cosmic force.

A new Western movement will consciously choose this world, and then will be immediately awed by the realization that it possesses immense powers to transform it. It will recognize that following this trail, a new stream of spiritual enlightenment comes into being: a more complex non-duality of intertwined emptiness and fullness. A Western awakening cannot but inherently include in it a renewed 'Bodhisattva vow': committing ourselves to evolve for the sake of this world and to forever strive to demolish all barriers between matter and spirit, we move the divine center of gravity towards our interiors, towards the heart of matter itself, until there's really nowhere to go: 'up there' is 'here' and 'here' is 'up there'

At present the New Age movement is far too decentralized and scattered to be regarded as a genuine movement. This may sound to some as a great pluralistic condition, and it is indeed great in regard to the rainbow of streams and voices. In the gay movement, the feminist movement or the human rights movement there are also various lucid voices, but this does not mean they have no mutual conventions, leading authorities and generalised outlines of credo.

In contrast, the New Age movement has no centers of attention and energy. It seems that this perplexes no one. So isn't it time to gather our forces into some synergistic and creative movement? Why do we confuse the aloofness of the subjective spirit with the awkward separateness of different energy centers? How come we, unlike other human movements, are not driven by the blessed impulse that brings together people with similar hopes and visions? The answer, again, may be our fear-driven avoidance of human culture.

Many take delight in claiming that a world-wide mass awakening takes place within the human mind, but there's surely no visibility of those masses. It seems like we're masses that hide pretty well, doing our best to be as harmless and ineffective as possible, somewhere in the uncharted territories of society's margins.

To defend ourselves, we pull out the spiritual concept of aloneness, as if the aloneness of the divine self might somehow get damaged the moment it is being called to share itself in an actual engaging process. Even for our isolated journey we could have benefited much from having a supportive movement. And claiming that any effort to create a collective will inevitably result in a destructive cultish tyranny is also quite odd in face of so many other movements which manage to sustain an extremely high level of individual independence, and at the same time demonstrate the amazing influential power of those who come together.

It is high time for us to consider a Western spiritual movement that will have its very own democratic institutions and elected leadership, educational structures and schools, academies and awards, prominent textbooks and integrated knowledge. Just like any other human movement, we should have our thinkers and our activists, our speakers and our educators.

A movement of this kind will possess its own general credo, a common philosophical ground, a paradigm that is heavily exposed to re-examination and international gatherings that will lay out the joined future visions. By its very nature, this kind of movement can sprout only from the recognition that there is a next step for the New Age culture and that this next step includes our coming out to the bright front-stage of human culture. This is a natural step, after the notion of individual sovereignty has been efficiently embedded and established: now we may fathom that individuality in itself, with no objective and external context, can become a new form of misery.

An international congress for an authentic Western spirituality should emerge out of this exulted understanding; a congress, consisting of the truly interested schools of thought, that will grope for some mutual ground in order to redefine our 21st Western spirituality and enlightenment.

It shouldn't be the kind of gatherings in which only mystics and esoteric teachers are allowed to speak out - it must blend with the new intriguing colors of activists, philosophers, scientists and visionaries, otherwise it might drown in abstraction and remain unshaken. It would be beneficial if our arguments piled up, and the artificial all-inclusive acceptance shattered - we do need fiery passion in order for us to spin together towards a substantive construction of our own unique spirituality.

Chapter Nine:

The Dark Side of the Western Spirit

*Read about the dark side of the Western spirit – its inclination towards materialism, consumerism, bourgeoisie and convenience * How this great downside has flattened our spirituality and has shaped it as an 'instant' culture.*

> "The ultimate goal of technology, the *telos* of *techne*, is to replace a natural world that's indifferent to our wishes — a world of hurricanes and hardships and breakable hearts, a world of resistance — with a world so responsive to our wishes as to be, effectively, a mere extension of the self".
>
> [Jonathan Franzen, writer]

At this stage we can already appreciate some of Western culture's most precious gifts that may assist us in laying the grounds for our new spirituality. First and foremost, it equips us with the scientific-objective-logical mind along with its highly effective structures of philosophical lineage (we'll go into this supreme gift in chapters ten and eleven). The second empowering gift is the tremendous emphasis on individual sovereignty and the freedom to create one's own life (as discussed at length in the fifth chapter). The third endowment, presented in the seventh chapter, is the ever-unfolding dynamic which manifests in the many qualities of ambition and motivation, improvement and change, inquisitiveness and healthy skepticism, evolutionary tension and the infinite creative enterprise. A fourth inspiration is in embracing the material universe and validating and affirming life. The last gift is the individual psychology (see fourth chapter), which helps unveil unconscious drives and thus dispose of blockages that might hinder the consolidation of the far more complex, new enlightenment.

However, everything comes at a price: the Western culture seems to be forever shadowed by its dark side, a most destructive side - perhaps worse than destructive, as destructiveness still bears some potential energy, *decadent*. The leaning towards individual sovereignty also attracts commerciality, consumerism and eclecticism; the ever-unfolding dynamic evokes a hunt for endless improvement, convenience and bourgeois comfort. Passionate inclination towards the objective world and the life-affirming embrace of the material cosmos turns into a blind obsession for the pleasure and drama of the objective world, thus making it extremely hard to detach the mind from the world of relationships and external gratification.

This multifaceted downside of Western culture, in which embracing matter becomes a materialistic view of life, leaves us depleted, with very little energy for any level of transformation, be it individual or collective. For this reason, it demands a discussion of its own.

But before going into it, it is important to remind ourselves that we shouldn't be carried away by some regressive, pre-modern fantasy of disdain for commerciality and dismissing money. The way to remedy and balance shortcomings is not to wish for the collapse of the entire mechanism - the West is by its nature materialistic and thus its spirituality has to be tied in with money. Part of engaging in the Western culture is to cultivate cultural critique; only when one isolates himself does he turn his back on the entire structure and wish the whole thing to disintegrate completely. Assuming that we no longer wish to avoid our culture, let us pinpoint destructive influences of Western materialism on our fragilely evolving spirituality.

Let's begin with commerciality, consumerism and eclecticism, which follow like a shadow the free-to-choose individual. As with everything else in our culture, so it happens that spirituality has turned into a vast mega-market of countless possibilities, all of them presented as commodities, trying to catch the eye of their overwhelmed potential consumer.

Before you know it, all differences between profound, elitist notions and radical complex systems and the most superficial, common clichés and simplistic (on the verge of silly) methods become blurred as they are all piled up on the same shelf. The overly generous pluralistic idea that it is all basically the 'same one and only truth' makes it impossible to tell the difference between Gurdjieff and any common copywriter who exclaims 'Be here and now!' The hazy seeker of truth wanders from here to there, picking a tremendous truth in one hand and a comforting spirituality book of 'flatland' in his other hand. Moreover, in our internet age *information* and *knowledge* are being amassed together, so one can no longer separate the wheat from the chaff.

In this atmosphere it is inevitably very hard not only to recognize the truer and the higher but also to deeply commit to any longer and demanding process or journey. At every given moment one can 'zap' and switch the channel, so the eye gets only to read the catchy headline without ever probing into the depths. There are many who go every second weekend for a totally different workshop or teacher, trying this or that while occasionally getting some 'awesome experience', as if spiritual engagement is a Luna-park attraction. And it is all followed by the natural habit of the consumer - to get easily bored and agitated, to quickly give up and move on only because it doesn't 'feel good'.

The problem is that too often not feeling good is actually a great indication of an opportunity to self-overcome. Wanting only to follow what we 'feel like' at the moment while elegantly avoiding unpleasant feelings can be one of the greatest spiritual pitfalls, when we take into account that any genuine path is destined to push many of our automatic 'buttons'. But due to the seductive commercial air, an unconscious association between the 'pleasant' and the 'true' is being ingrained in our brains, suppressing the spiritual truth that physical comfort and pleasure are quite often a hindrance while physical discomfort frequently drives one towards transcendence of both body and mind.

The supposedly free individual, who has now turned into an unconsciously enslaved consumer, gradually loses his patience. After all, the agitated consumer of the West has no time; rushing from here to there, the spiritual engagement is nothing but a relieving stop on his way. Frantically he looks for the easiest and quickest paths (or rather for some no-path path); he seeks for some explosive 'miracle' that happens with a minute effort on his part; he expects to be excited, to be extraordinarily touched, to be intensely stimulated as if spirituality was a refined form of entertainment.

Spiritual authorities become in his eyes but salesmen while he, the consumer, warily inspects their merchandise. There is a constant lookout for the next thing, the next retreat or the new teacher, since nothing can live up to one's expectations. The greatest miracle of them all is, of course, instant enlightenment, an enlightenment achieved in one glance or in one brief moment of 'sincere inquiry'. Its popular suppliers readily backup this possibility, heavily focusing on the encapsulated moment of revelation and accordingly proclaiming the awakening of several people in one retreat.

Even prominent teachers are tempted to putting on a show, 'performing' enlightenment instead of being it with honest simplicity; sometimes they might find themselves making unrealistic promises, and even becoming subtly manipulative in fear of losing their success to the powerful and cynical market forces.

Indeed, we have long since separated from the times in which mythological devoted seekers were fervently climbing the Himalayas, leaving the whole world behind in the hope of finding the one true teacher who would disclose the highest truth (of course, after having tested them vehemently and even putting to test their sincerity through unbearable demands).

The meticulous meditative processes of the past are now reduced to childish expectation for peak experience that would miraculously 'end it all' right here right now. Enlightenment is to be acquired through money and the mere random visit at the Satsang hall. Naturally, this spirit of consumerism allures people who realize they can turn their own enlightened glimpses and fragmented knowledge into a promising career.

This is one more catalyst for the flattening of the majestic traditional lineages of the East. The basic truth, that any genuinely liberated teacher would adhere to, is that the rarity of enlightened ones hasn't changed throughout the ages, and there are no far reaching implications for the increase of peak experience in workshops and retreats.

Another distressing example for the way consumerism has re-shaped spirituality itself is the enormous popularity of the 'law of attraction'. Harnessing spirituality in order to persuade the universe to deliver us our desired materialistic aims is nothing but an extension of Western materialism. The notion of drawing 'abundance' into our lives is deviously blended into the superiority and precedence of consciousness and even enlightenment itself.

Commerciality inevitably limits spiritual depths. It molds the knowledge as a commodity, learning how to respond well enough to the consumer's demands such as 'What would it give me?' and 'How soon would that work?' The moment spirituality is entwined around money and publicity it is allured by the temptation to flatten itself in order to adjust to mass marketing. In this kind of climate, the forces of the market are the ones to select from the depths of knowledge whatever seems to be appropriate for bestselling books and crowded workshops. Messages become slogans, short and superficial, in order to reach 'as many people as possible'. Spirituality becomes ingratiating and flattering, and any trace of demanding complexity is elegantly removed from the display window. Allowing the forces of the market to define and shape our spirituality is hazardous in so many respects.

Above all, the spiritual consumer finds himself struggling with the wondrous gift of freedom of choice, trying to fathom, now that he can do whatever he wants, what it is exactly that he *really* wants; he is supposed to know and actually invent his own direction, and this is precisely where freedom of choice can turn us into perplexed consumers, instead of conscious creators. The much sought-after choice hands us the burden of responsibility, though in the process we might get dizzy and lose our way. Indeed, it is highly important to acknowledge the dual nature of choice, to become wary of hasty conclusions such as 'since it doesn't make me feel good, it cannot be right for me', and to avoid the tempting flightiness enabled by our freedom of choice as it robs us of our other freedom - to deeply delve into more demanding forms of knowledge, even if they require years of steadfast learning.

The hunt for endless improvement, convenience and bourgeois comfort is yet another barrier to transcend. One of the greatest drives of Western society, to ever-improve the quality of life, brought about the danger of feeling too cozy. When everything is too good, too available, we easily forget what life is all about, so we sink into an oblivious bourgeoisie, conveniently settling down to a degree that we no longer feel the painful urge to go beyond our present way of living. Our society is over-satiated, highly smug, and only the rare few can actually connect with the wonderful dissatisfaction of evolutionary tension in this kind of climate. Since so many of us are lacking in material hardship and life is externally easy-going, it's hard to find within oneself the immense energy required for transcending the material world and even before that, the fundamental urge to leave behind such a world.

We acutely lack the sufficient energy for a revolution, be it internal or external. We lack that precious restless passion that wants to turn the whole world upside down. And since even a great deal of our psychological suffering is a made-up suffering, formed out of boredom and pampering, even that is not powerful enough to drive us towards the gateway of inner revolution. In this atmosphere, a too taxing effort is out of the question, so we keep looking for easier substitutes, suppressing our deep knowledge that to truly transform one often must go through intense and even horrible tests of both body and mind.

In such a convenient world, one must creatively set for himself challenges of self-overcoming and an environment steeped in evolutionary tension. In many respects, we have to lead in the West an idealistic and somewhat 'subversive' life, extremely critical of the bourgeois within ourselves. Being supported by great and unpleasant awakeners such as Gurdjieff and Krishnamurti, and being suspicious of those authorities who wish only to please and comfort us, can be quite beneficial. Those who make us feel too good and cozy are often those who have been tempted themselves to indulge the consumer's lower needs.

Lastly, we have to consider the blind obsession for the pleasure and drama of the objective world. Ingrained in the Western spirit is the compulsive bias towards the world of objects, which obstructs our way to spiritual depths. On the one hand, we have too much leisure time, which allows us to sink into self-created dramas of stormy relationships and intense emotionalism that protect us from the emptiness and meaninglessness of our present life. Divorced from any grand vision or broad context that could have provided us with some higher cosmic drama, we tirelessly nourish an illusory intense relationship with the world. On the other hand, nourishing so enthusiastically the world of objects, we end up with the ironic feeling that we have no time. Juggling our countless commitments, we are hardly able to embrace spiritual engagement as something more than a hobby, and therefore are incapable of stabilizing spiritual depths in our lives.

We are so addicted to the pleasure of objects, that we finally turn even the notion of enlightenment into the promise of absolute enjoyment; that is, feeling good *all the time*. Unconsciously we seek for enlightenment as if it was just another object to pursue, thus blending the will to feel good and the transcendent identity to a degree that we can no longer get in touch with the true nature of liberation.

Instead, we should learn how to use the frenzy of the illusory Western haunt for externals as a new platform for liberation. Gathering our own individual forces in order to at least partially renounce the world, and also withdrawing from the self-created drama and superficial indulgence, can help us take in the many benefits of the Western spirit while pushing away its darker side of obsession and compulsion.

Chapter Ten:

Whatever Happened to Logic?

Read how we have turned our backs on our own scientific mind and have sunk into the world of abstractions – and how embracing the Western's systematic and logical view can dramatically change our spirituality for the better

> "What is the religious mind? And what is the scientific mind? I feel those are the only two real minds that can resolve the problems of the world. The really scientific mind is... the logical mind, the mind that can think clearly, freely, without prejudice, without fear, can investigate into the whole problem of matter, life and speed and so on. Can that mind enter into the religious mind, or are they two different things? The religious mind is the mind that in no way follows tradition, that is utterly free from all authority; it is not investigating from a centre as knowledge, as the scientific spirit does. When the scientific mind breaks through the limitations of knowledge, then perhaps it approaches the religious mind".

[Jiddu Krishnamurti, spiritual teacher and philosopher]

Logic is the effortful attempt to attain an ordered, systematic and well-reasoned understanding of reality by means of an intellectual probing. Being such an inquisitive and object-oriented spirit, it is no wonder that logic was embraced by the Western society as its directing compass. Steadily cultivated by ancient civilizations such as India and China, and reaching astonishing magnitudes in ancient Greece (eventually formalized by Aristotle), it has finally become the foundation of the Western scientific endeavor. Science, the body of reliable knowledge - the one that can be logically and rationally explained - has become for the last five hundred years the vibrating core of the Western spirit. Without logic, without the ability to inquire into the validity of modes of reasoning and forms of arguments, there could be no ground for the testability of arguments through experimentation and empirical observation.

Though historically practiced in several schools of spiritual thought - Socrates, for instance, was a great rationalist mystic - logic is not too welcome in the New Age worlds. The mere term 'rational mysticism' might sound to the New Age ear like an oxymoron. Committing to build careful and systematic claims and to make sound intellectual observations does not seem to be part and parcel of the spiritual journey, both for speakers and listeners.

There is even some ingrained pride about it - as if the spiritual is beyond the rational commitment, as if being trans-rational (beyond ordinary linear thought) one no longer needs to care about minor details such as sensibility and coherence. Logic, so we are told by our spiritual elders, somehow stands in contrast to the spiritual being, and the two might only randomly intersect. It is definitely not an imperative condition, either for individual transformation or the evolution of the spirit at large.

Indeed, everyone is guided in their first steps along the spiritual trail to abandon their 'head' and sink into their 'heart'; Western seekers are humorously and compassionately teased for their incessant need to 'understand' that which is 'beyond understanding'. We easily confuse the 'head' of repetitive psychological thoughts (actually, emotions in disguise) and the arrogant and cunning mind with the 'head' of wakeful inquiry that demands to go to the bottom of things, and justifiably expects systematic coherence in a culture reigned by the scientific spirit for more than five hundred years.

Of course, one can only guess the unconscious horror of a spiritual master who must face a probing mind, that lurks for every apparent contradiction in the teaching - to which the most automatic response will be 'just surrender' or 'silence your mind and be here and now'.

The common conception is that mysticism by its very nature entails abstractions - words can never 'describe' or 'contain' - which is true only in some respects. In so many other respects it is completely possible to consolidate a comprehensive and structured spiritual knowledge without elusive, somewhat romantic contradictions; it is also possible (and vital) to clearly interpret the meanings and implications of any transcendental experience. Another illogical tendency is attributing disproportionate significance to the subjective experience and view, as if it was the most objective reality (for example, 'the world is an illusion'), while totally neglecting the fact that all subjective experience takes place within an objective and observable universe and as part of large-scale processes. We tend to give a higher validity to non-empirical subjective experiences, such as intuition, 'gut feeling' and inner visions, as if they were all true just because we trust them to be true. Carelessly we espouse unfounded notions, which are clearly independent of any logical frame of reference; believing and trusting are enough to make something 'true', thus we give an absolute value to so many relative 'truths' - especially when these truths are handed to us by 'unquestionable' authorities.

Absolutism and abstraction are definitely good ways to avoid undermining discussions. Committing oneself to coherence obviously gets one into the trouble of merciless self-inquiry, and realizing that our subjective feelings are not enough to validate anything implies that we can never be uncritically content with our knowledge of reality.

Suppressing our logical-objective mind entraps us in a hazy world of abstractions, unexamined beliefs and baseless ideas. Naturally this withholds the evolution of our New Age movement. By turning our backs on the scientific spirit, we prevent its blessed diffusion into our spiritual worlds, a diffusion which could enable the greatest leap of them all. So now we should take a look at four major ways in which logic and scientific spirit can transform our sprouting spirituality.

A supremely important characteristic of the scientific spirit is the weariless *destabilization of paradigm*. Even the most cherished paradigms, which are carefully cultivated for hundreds of years of increasing conviction, can all at once collapse in the face of some new evidence or one genius insight. Of course, this is enabled by the sacred and humble knowing that the search for truth is unending by its very nature, and no matter how progressive we feel we are, "what we see as today's wholes may very well become tomorrow's parts" (Ken Wilber).

For example, the highly admired Newtonian universe partially collapsed the moment Einstein introduced his groundbreaking theories, but Einstein's own yearning for a unified field theory was thwarted by the advancing quantum physics (among other factors). It is immanent in science that one force rises up for some time and then another overpowers it, since it contains more truth in it - there is a constant 'competition' which does not only undermine previous truths but actually leaves only that which is stable enough to further build upon. An infinite journey towards the theory of everything enkindles the already flaring heart of every new scientist.

Disappointingly enough, in spirituality it is far from being the case. Spiritual ideas are enshrined, sometimes for thousands of years, and what keeps them so untouched is the great misconception that since truth is eternal, whatever was true two thousand years ago will be true also in two thousand years from now. This implies that one shouldn't question the paradigm itself, since antiquity is an eternal proof of validity.

This presupposition is puzzling, given the fact that just like science, subjective inquiry into the mysteries of life is far from being revelatory enough to satiate our hungry minds. If we listen attentively, perhaps we would hear the call of the universal spirit itself - to be prepared to ask frightfully dangerous questions that might turn the spiritual paradigm upside down.

Spirituality and spiritual enlightenment must be susceptible to a daring questioning just like all other fields of human knowledge. Believing that one should not make bold judgments and revolutionary distinctions - because using the head is missing the target - is an enormous obstruction on our way.

This is also why any kind of gathering of spiritual authorities seems to be so hopelessly futile: unlike scientists, who know they all share the perpetual quest for the complete truth and are thus capable of holding fruitful dialogues, spiritual teachers are convinced that they have already found the absolute truth, so what's the point of stimulating a discussion? Their teaching is already eloquently arranged and anyway, whatever they think or say is derived from the absolute truth in which they are fully immersed.

The only way out from this predicament is letting go of the belief that one abides in some final truth, since whatever it is that we have found is by the very nature of our brains a confined and relative revelation. One should not confuse the realization of the divine self with the all-encompassing truth about the mysteries of life, in light of which all spiritual truths are mere theories and all 'final realizations' are but minor immersions.

In science there are *evolving lineages*, while in the spiritual world we have static lineages. While the scientific lineages consist of passionate quarrels based on sufficient respect, explicitly for the sake of the progress towards truth, spiritual lineages hold dear pre-modern knowledge and are expected to preserve it - at the most, the successors are allowed to adjust terminology and rhetoric for the new generations. The greatness and divinity of the forefathers is being sanctified to a degree that one simply cannot formulate or utter earth-shaking new ideas (otherwise he parts from his lineage).

Espousing the scientific tradition of evolving lineages is not meant to aid us in feeling more belonging to some great heritage, but rather in communicating with a continuum of knowledge, to which we refer and to which we add new arguments and updates. For this aim, we should greatly broaden our New Age library, including in it not only the heavily repetitive Yogic and Taoist knowledge but also the buzzing, disquieting hive of Western philosophy: from Socrates to Nietzsche, from Foucault to Einstein.

In this way we can add new intricacies of colors and stimulants beyond Eastern abstractions. As Westerners we can take pride in having such a glorious tradition of independent thinkers, and becoming knowledgeable in this field can enrich us in so many ways.

Even the mere contemplation on turning the New Age movement into an authentic Western spirituality, which serves as part of the greater Western philosophical knowledge, might elicit from within a brand new energy. In fact, this may be just the right time to merge our spirituality with philosophy, transforming it into some 'direct ontology'. In this light, spiritual teachers can be regarded as 'direct philosophers', who live on the frontier between academy and mysticism, and a new generation of spiritual aspirants will freely float between logic and liberation, science and subjective revelation.

In science everything is continuously being put to test and whatever prevails is that which proves a *systematic coherence* which clearly overcomes the systematic coherence of its competitors. Science's noble aspiration to objectively observe processes stands in stark contrast with the spiritual leaning, which tends to attribute absolute validity to the subjective, and thus too often rejects any attempts to be looked at in the context of large-scale processes (which might undermine beliefs and 'inner convictions').

For evolution's sake, spiritual claims and methods must undergo decisive methodical processing and actual testing. Spirituality can and should afford disposing of anything that doesn't withstand these tests, so it gradually becomes academically stable, logically arranged, measurable and empirical. Testing claims and methods empirically and clinically is a great purification process, which can reveal the specific values and degrees of influence of this or that.

At the same time, whenever some esoteric and mystical element (for instance, subtle bodies such as chakras and fields, or the reality of reincarnation) is meticulously and systematically proven, it will be integrated into our comprehensive canon of knowledge, as we do not forego the esoteric but only the blind belief in it.

In this way, we will finally move away from the elusive and misty world of 'intuitions' and 'inner convictions' and develop a meticulous, pristine science of consciousness, which will become a tremendous contribution to our human culture.

Shifting from enlightenment as a subjective world-view into a genuine science is a potent move. For example, knowledge of Kundalini can be easily organized by comparing the various models until one unified model consolidates. There are enough exciting similarities, which hold the power to create scientific coherence, and we must not fear the contradictions which strive to defeat each other, since this is how science works. Examining which is more systematically consistent, in an ecstatic process of trial and error, will finally turn enlightenment into a non-abstract, highly detectable phenomenon.

This leads us to one last scientific axiom which can wonderfully support us in our effort to crystallize Western spirituality: in science *you cannot afford to see what you wish to see*. Drawing again from Einstein's life story, in the last thirty years of his lifetime he insisted, quite religiously, that there are governing rules of the universe which are steady and all-prevailing, so he persistently endeavored to develop his unified field theory in spite of the growing evidence of quantum physics' unpredictability - yet he couldn't prove his point, no matter how hard he believed in it.

Embracing this overwhelmingly strict rule in spiritual thought can help develop a higher level of the spiritual imperative 'see things as they are': if all claims, no matter how 'sacred' they are, are ruthlessly examined in a logical context, an intense purification will begin to take place and all distortions caused by the wish to see something that is really not there will be demolished.

Our hidden motivation that drives us towards unexamined assertions will be easily unveiled, as an impulse of survival which prompts us to 'see' meaning and purpose in anything that happens; to enshrine ourselves, away from this empty universe, in self-made sanctuaries of beliefs, hopes and comforts.

Intuition is a good thing, yet it is only a good starting point. Through intuition we can correctly pick up on logical possibilities, worthy candidates that might become a stable logical formula. But then, cutting through the mist of projections and prejudice caused by the psychological need to 'see' something, the intuition must make its way through stormy and vehement procedure of verification in order to reach the bright world of pure logic.

In such a world one cannot simply 'believe' in the consistent power of positive thinking, prayer, miracles or alternative medicine, because one really wants to know the truth, even when the truth leaves him naked in the darkest space.

Chapter Eleven:

The Great March of Evolution

*Read how Darwin's evolution which has practically shaken to the core all the foundations of Western thought can do the same with our spirituality * Then explore what really happens when we steep spirituality in the ever-unfolding evolutionary context.*

> "We need a new theology of the cosmos - one that is grounded in the best science of our day. It will be a theology in which God is very present precisely *in* all the dynamism and patterns of the created order. A theology of evolution sees God as deeply involved in the evolutionary process of the world. God is making the world by means of evolution. And the evolutionary process in its turn is seen as striving toward God... God is Self-expressing and Self-realizing in evolution".
>
> [Beatrice Bruteau, philosopher]

It has all begun, at least so it seems, with Darwin.

Elegantly skipping the finer details of his biological revolution, *essentially* what Darwin did was ingeniously demonstrate the fact that evolution possesses its own inner forces, forces which need not be monitored by some external organizing element. These inner forces, we can further deduce, are also those which have molded the complex human being - the one being that is capable of observing the entire evolutionary process and inquiring into it. With Darwin, even the human, who for some reason had been customarily perceived as distinguished from the rest of the material process - being specially originated from a divine or spiritual source - became an inseparable part of this organic process of perpetual growth.

The tragically misunderstood Nietzsche was the first one to comprehend the magnitude of the evolutionary revolution in regard to its psychological and philosophical implications. Nietzsche's attempt at delineating a new path of Godless psycho-spiritual evolution was daringly experimental and highly disputable, yet its fingerprints; conscious and even more so unconscious, are clearly evident in our secular culture to this day.

While the 19th century served as the womb silently growing the new paradigm within it, the beginning of the 20th century was an eruption of this world-view reversal. Following this biological earthquake, other scientific fields started to infuse coinciding discoveries. Freud eloquently demonstrated that inner forces within the mind propagate human psychology. With Freud, these forces of projection and suppression, desire and concealment finally took the place of the demonic and angelic characters that humans had used to imaginatively struggle with in pre-modern past. Psychology was finally recognized as an inner dynamics which is to be resolved only through man's relationship with his own self.

Simultaneously, in physics and cosmology Einstein finally dared to take the step which his predecessors had only groped: he dismissed absolute time and absolute space, thus liberating the universe from absolute elements which had confined it for eons, unveiling a relative inner activity independent of any external factor.

Unintentionally, and against his own stubbornly held perceptions of reality, he eventually brought about the ascent of quantum physics. This bothersome avalanche of discoveries revealed Heisenberg's uncertainty principle and worse, bewildering relative interrelation between the observer and the observed universe. Einstein's relative physics, Heisenberg's mathematics of uncertainty and Gödel's philosophical incompleteness have all contributed to the reconstruction of a subjective, non-absolute cosmos.

Another line of scientific thought also began unfolding through the awe-inspiring works of the 'spiritual evolution' advocates, who started infusing biological evolution with spirit. This long chain of scientists and philosophers - such as geologist De Chardin, philosopher Rudolf Steiner, the more contemporary philosopher Beatrice Bruteau, cosmologist Brian Swimme and philosopher Ken Wilber - ascribed a spiritual tendency to evolution and the unfolding universe.

Matter, forever forming from within itself, was to be perceived as a movement of the spirit which aspires to create ever increasing complexities in order to attain one day an 'omega point', a point of total transmutation into spirit which is the concealed drive of the entire evolutionary process. This theory of spiritual evolution has not only granted a deeper value to evolving matter but has endowed with direction and purpose the seemingly blind forces of evolution.

Again, Nietzsche's fingerprints are also evident in the 20th century torrent of postmodernism and relativism. Postmodernism, the great reaction to scientific and objective efforts to explain reality, brilliantly suggested that reality is merely constructed as the mind tries to understand its own personal reality, which implies that reality only comes into being through our *interpretation* of what the world means to us individually. This fallibility of any definite 'reality' is further supported by relativism, which upends all absolute truth, claiming that truth is always relative to some particular frame of reference.

Add to these outrageous philosophical and scientific shifts, which have so dramatically interpenetrated our culture and personal minds, the two world wars that completely eroded all 'isms' and definitive ideologies, the stormy rebellion of the sixties, the impressive triumphs of the human rights movements, the growing sanctification of the freedom of speech and individual world-view, and the crumbling of authoritative figures, from parents to journalists who, due to the Internet, are no longer perceived to be the exclusive messengers of 'objective' information.

All of these cultural influxes are, essentially, one and the same revolution in human thought, a revolution that is made of two intertwined giant leaps: the universe has revealed itself as an inner dynamic, which needs no externally organizing presence - it is a self-generating, self-sustaining dynamic. Out of the implied and inevitable shattering of the greatest absolute of them all - the external God - all other smaller absolutes have turned to dust: time, space, the universe's objectivity, the external forces that seemed to shape the human psyche, the spirit as an entity unto itself (separated from matter), truth and authority.

Should this revolution interfere with our spirituality in the slightest? For thousands of years the fundamental axiom of spirituality has been precisely the conviction that the regions of the spirit (and therefore the spiritual revelation) are to remain by their very nature eternally unaffected by all the upheavals of time and becoming.

Of course, this is a sound argument. And yet, shouldn't we attempt in the face of an emerging new universe, at least as part of some thought experiment, to overturn this dogma? Perhaps this is also the time for a paradigm shift in our Western spirituality, allowing the diffusion of deconstructive elements to carry us too into a non-absolute evolutionary process. For some reason we assume that a spirituality that knew nothing of 20th century cosmology - the ever-expanding universe with its more than one hundred and seventy billion galaxies - can peacefully make its way into the 21st century and claim perfect relevance. Thus we must ponder: is there no update of our spirituality considering the stunning discoveries of the nature of the universe and planet earth with its human inhabitants?

How can Darwin's evolution, which has shaken to the core all of the West's thought structures, reshape our spirituality? What takes place when we imbue spiritual revelation with the ever-unfolding evolutionary context? Couldn't there be as a result a total upending of interpretation as to what spirituality really means?

The most immediate thing that occurs when we allow the crumbling of all absolutes and constants in the field of spirituality is that divinity can no longer hover apathetically and neutrally outside the universe. Rather, it transforms into an evolving and expanding divinity, completely whole in itself yet incomplete and somehow dependent on the becoming of the universe as its *own* process of becoming.

This makes for a totally different, far more complex non-duality: if there is really only one, there cannot be a universe and a divinity; assuming that God is external and unaffected is a dual perception. This implies that the becoming universe is in effect the becoming God. If the universe is ever-expanding, this necessarily means that God is ever-expanding, and if human consciousness is evolving, this means that God's own consciousness evolves.

God is not waiting for us somewhere at the end of the road, but rather tirelessly unfolds as an accelerating cosmos, bubbling up as dark matter, atoms and molecules to surpass its own primordial state. Naturally, this instills an enormous divine value into the only apparently material cosmos.

Depending on the observer, this holds within it either a dreadful or elating implications: since the infinite, ever-expanding evolution is the divine itself, there's no more spiritual reason to hope to ever go anywhere else; we're not going to 'return' to the Lord or dissipate into Nirvana as God himself does not want to reverse to its original formless state. There are no two separated planes of reality, a relative one and an absolute one, and with that understanding the ancient split between matter and spirit can die out.

A Western spirituality might thus develop its own complex non-duality, which incorporates evolution and the changing universe into divinity. This kind of non-duality will finally align the Western tendency to embrace the evolving world with the eternal beat of spiritual yearning. The pre-modern notion which asserts that the 'relative' and 'temporary' world pales into insignificance in the face of divine transcendence will be replaced with a profound sanctification of the becoming universe.

All at once it will seem plausible to form a spirituality based upon the visible universe alone - and by doing so, the subtle form of tormenting split within the Western spiritual aspirant will come to an end. Needless to say, such a revolution, such a paradigm turnover, will cause spiritually what Einstein and Bohr did to Newton's perfectly static and deterministic universe - in our context, the Newtonic universe of spirituality is the never-changing divine reality which peacefully hovers over our ever-changing universe.

Following the previous thought experiment, we might also daringly question whether our spiritual capacities stem organically from the Darwinian evolution. If biological evolution is correct, this means that we humans are not distinguished from all other processes as we are no longer considered special beings who fell from the heavens into this material world. Without divine human origin this might imply that our consciousness, even its spiritually evolved layers, has come into being from within matter, just like a flower or a tree.

Just as the capacity of self-consciousness emerged from physics, chemistry and biology, so did the soul, the chakras, the subtle layers of consciousness and perhaps reincarnation. Evolution thus becomes increasingly sublimated, gradually turning from the evolution of matter to the evolution of the refined materials of our consciousness. In this context spirituality is the universe developing higher cognitive skills, and humans are but conscious extensions of the cosmos - its awakening mind.

This is a new evolutionary context, in which the divine self increasingly glows out of matter in an awesomely gradual process of becoming. To become enlightened means then to be a particle of matter that has managed to develop the capacity of total universal cognition, as if the whole universe has opened a giant eye through one's mind.

Enlightenment in this frame of reference is a material transmutation, just like Jiddu Krishnamurti postulated, so perhaps in the future we will be able to demystify the enlightened process in the same way that science managed to explain thunder, which had been considered customarily as the play of angry Gods.

What are the possible consequences of this paradigm shift? The most obvious one, of course, is that as evolution liberates us from the need for a supporting and directing external being, we can finally realize that as humanity we have outgrown the habitual dependency on God's embrace. We will be able to renounce the imaginary pre-modern parts of our spirituality which have brought about the dependent belief in forces beyond creation. Once and for all we will be able to rid ourselves of superstitions, such as attributing divine will to man-made disasters in the world; it will be clear as daylight that all human actions result from levels of development and not from the handiwork of some invisible puppeteer.

By truly allowing the external God to die - and as a result to silently watch the death of religious narratives and mythologies, moral values and lawful impediments - there will be only the divine self rising from within evolution, dusting down the old notions of truth and redefining truth and meaning. Without grace, a profound maturation awaits us, realizing that since it's only us now, there's no reason to wait and hope. We are the source of all grace and benediction, and with this consolidation of total responsibility, it will be obvious that 2012 is us taking our fate in our own hands. *We are 2012*.

The expansion of consciousness in an evolutionary context is not about shirking the human experience but rather it is about and for the expansion of the human experience itself. Now that consciousness is no longer a focal point of rest or a subtle means of escape, it transforms into a tremendous force at the service of human's further development. It is revealed as the key that can connect matter and spirit and thus amazingly empower the search for new solutions to our collective dilemmas and crises. The moment consciousness is regarded not as a mystical point of reference for the sake of personal self-observation but as an evolutionary tool, humanity will know that consciousness is the prime and inexhaustible resource of this planet.

And when the spiritual revelation stops acting as the eternal and neutral outsider and begins its diffusion into the engaging world, even liberation will be viewed as the creation of new models of humans; new future mutations to inspire further development.

In effect there are no two evolutions after all. The scientific and academic evolution of the West and the evolution of consciousness through genuine spiritual practice are only seemingly separated. In reality, this has always been only one evolutionary flow in which each stream serves in the development of either its subjective aspect or its objective aspect.

In other words, the emergence of such great individuals as Darwin and Nietzsche is just as significant as the appearance of Jiddu Krishnamurti and Ramana Maharishi. In this light, spiritual mastery should be viewed as a genius in the field of consciousness, in the same manner that we as humanity consider great minds in their unique fields of expertise, such as in physics, psychology or any other science.

This equal vision, which includes all great minds on one scale of evolutionary flow, will finally place spiritual enlightenment in its proud yet humble seat, alongside all other fields of human excellence. As a consequence, each personal enlightenment will be understood as one more stepping stone in the general process of humanity's growth. Enlightenment then will not be the promise of a final point of rest but the marking of our present frontier of consciousness, which one day will be breached too, thus opening up new horizons of limitless possibilities.

Chapter Twelve:

Our Credo

What will the credo of an authentic Western spirituality look like? * After eleven chapters of destruction and re-construction – an initial and groping effort to outline the fundamentals of our new emerging spirituality.

When an individual wishes to liberate himself, he must first become aware of all the different influences, conscious and even more so unconscious, that have molded and conditioned his personality. Becoming fully conscious of each influence is the first necessary step which enables a sufficient degree of disassociation; a disassociation that allows the individual to disengage himself from the detrimental influences and at the same time to reassume, now deliberately and willingly, the favorable aspects of these influences.

In the same way, learning about the various influences that have given shape to the New Age movement, and the cultural and historical contexts in which this movement came into being, is compulsory if we ever hope to know what is a superfluous influence and what we should espouse wholeheartedly. Being automatic about the whole process which has forged our collective persona means that we are forever unconsciously swayed by strong forces which inhibit our long-awaited growth.

We, the individuals forming the New Age movement, are a mixture of influences and conditionings, both troublesome and beneficial. To come to terms with this state of affairs and face head on whatever awaits us in this collective subconscious, may not be a pleasant task.

Nevertheless, this has to be done - and this is why we underwent this bold exploration throughout the book. That is why I have persistently expounded the many intricate pros and cons of each influence: starting with the manifold gifts that have been showered on us by the Eastern spirit - along with its irrelevant dispositions and notions; then exploring the undesirable effects of the truly desirable psychological revolution; afterward, surveying the pre-modern religious impressions and the legacy of the authoritative spiritual mediator, and finally looking over the riches of Western culture alongside its major drawbacks.

The beautiful thing is that we need not dust down any kind of influence but rather wisely extricate their potential wisdom and use them flexibly and consciously. An authentic Western spirituality will freely draw goodness from all streams and cultures - Eastern spirituality, psychology, religions, Gurus, science, philosophy, capitalism, democracy and Western spirit - while rejecting their excesses and deficiencies.

Of course, there is a deep-rooted reason that has motivated us in the first place to wrongly use these many different concepts and inspirations. Back to the example of the individual liberation, when there is a measure of frailty and fear in the individual's heart he might cling to concepts that seem to keep him safe and unaffected. He might also misinterpret concepts in a way that is compatible with his deepest psychological needs. Correspondingly, the New Age movement has drawn from these tremendous streams of thought and knowledge only the elements that helped cover up the fear of Western life and the resulting avoidance ingrained within so many of its partakers. It has altered the original meanings and implications of some concepts so that they would be more soothing to the ear and soul.

The New Age movement has thus unknowingly developed a spirituality that is a mere reaction to the Western culture, and has in doing so created an unbridgeable split between itself and the rest of the world. The poor result is a stagnant predicament in which a whole movement - potentially with a tremendous power to change the world - stands aloof and neutral, proudly negating the world only to disguise its feeble lower three chakras.

Enveloped by supportive concepts - by a simplistic antithesis of everything that is held sacred in the Western culture - it has become incapable of hearing the cosmos' desperate call. For some, it seems somewhat romantic that most spiritual teachers and authorities who are overwhelmingly accepted among the spiritual aspirants' community, are almost outcasts in terms of general social affiliation. However, considering the potential effect of consciousness' teaching on the world at large this is hardly satisfactory.

Becoming aware of our collective subconscious of fears and conditionings, we might realize that aside from the purification of the individual psychological layers, there is yet one more layer which too often passes unnoticed: the New Age movement's stream of fearful misconceptions which anyone interested in spirituality nowadays is susceptible to 'catch', and to turn into its choiceless vehicle.

This hurdle that we're being asked to leap over makes a lot of sense when we take into account the thrilling fact that, as spiritual Westerners living in the 21st century, we are destined to bring about a much more complex and multi-faceted form of enlightenment, which includes the Eastern attainments yet unimaginably transcends them.

Naturally, our challenge is great, but knowing it is of paramount importance in the larger context of humanity's future, we can feel a cosmic urge bubbling from within us, quickening our pace. We cannot go back now to be protected and comforted by God, the Guru or some absolute Truth - we have gone too far. The raw material of our spirituality, the Godhead that is rising now from the depths of both matter and mind, has already become too unbridled, too apparent to ignore.

The New Age movement is not to be demolished in order to make space for some other powerful surge of spirituality. Rather, it should expand and evolve just like a tiny seed that holds within it the greater promise of a splendid tree. The term in itself contains all spiritual involvement that is secular, independent, individual, eclectic and free from lawful impediments.

Now that we're becoming conscious of our partaking in a larger movement of consciousness, however, this kind of activity has to be redefined as part of a greater effort to awaken the movement's urge for self-identity.

It will be good to 'do battle' with each other, in the framework of an international congress, until a new and more suitable term will come into being. In this manifesto I refer to it as the school of 'authentic Western spirituality', but this is just one, not-too-brilliant proposition. One way or the other, the fundamental idea is clear and simple: the New Age movement is transforming into a new form of Western spirituality, more established, more deeply rooted, more open-eyed and conscious of itself.

Realizing that indeed we're part of a great movement and all that is implied from it, and fighting over mutual terminology, is not something to belittle. This very act is the starting point of our transformation as a movement. At this stage we are so sadly decentralized and dispersed, lacking in the evolutionary urge to look for common grounds and fundamentals. Perhaps it is so because we hold on too passionately to the idea of being alone, but being alone never meant to be aloof and protectively separated. After all, we're long past the times in which belonging to a collective movement implied an immediate suffocation of one's individuality.

We live in wondrous times, not in relation to the unfounded promise of 2012 but rather because never in the history of mankind has there been such an abundant, filled-with-possibilities period. The progressive spirit which fervently promotes higher education, accessibility of all knowledge, freedom of speech and an excellent quality of life, is a most fertile ground for a future development that would break through the present gloomy dullness.

Of course, one should keep in mind that a revolution in today's world would not necessarily take the form of violent demonstrations in the town square. Like everything else that has been stripped down to its essentials, revolution nowadays can be purely a process of implanting new ideas into humanity's mind and heart. We should avoid preconditioned images that might interfere with the simplicity and directness of the process.

In our sleepy state even a negative dynamics of fierce polemic is welcome. When people become too lethargic, a terrible crisis could unexpectedly serve as a catalyst for a new awakening. For this reason, this entire manifesto has not been written in the hope that everyone would agree with me and immediately subscribe to every word I've written. Rather, it is the other way around: I have written it to enkindle a passionate discussion and new forms of action. That is why I have expressed the ideas with pathos, the likes of which was typical in historical manifests, untouched by the cynical air of today's world - for cynicism, the feeling that everything has already happened and that there's nothing new and surprising to breed, is the nemesis of all manifestos.

What will the credo of an authentic Western spirituality look like? After eleven chapters of destruction and re-construction, here is an initial and groping effort to delineate the ten fundamentals of our new emerging spirituality. Obviously, no man can define this credo alone - this is, after all, a collective enterprise - so these are only catalysts for a future dialogue.

1. *We choose - consciously, wholeheartedly, fearlessly and irreversibly - the Western life and all its challenges, however tormenting they may be.* For this noble - and yes, spiritual - purpose, we will dispose of any

psychological hindrance or conditioning that might alienate us from this life. This is our home and this is our spirit, and therefore our spirituality will not be molded as an antithesis of the Western life but rather as an updated 21st Western spirituality.

2. *We lovingly and gratefully espouse the gifts of Eastern spirituality* - self-effort as a most prominent fundamental, direct meditation as the central spiritual practice, non-duality as a frame of reference to all philosophies, divine self-identity and detailed maps of consciousness. These are all invaluable aids which empower us in our supreme wish to dedicate every breath we take to the development of consciousness, until consciousness is fully revealed as a seed of divinity which strives to break through from within us and

create the world anew. *Nonetheless, it is our Western duty to reject such notions as 'emptiness', 'world as illusion', 'ego annihilation', 'liberation from life', 'life as suffering', 'unconditional flow with life' and so on.* This terminology, along with its essential world-view, is not applicable to life in the West. Henceforth, we will do our best to produce a new terminology and a new world-view, through the power of our discerning mind, in order to better embrace the intricacies of the objective world. Furthermore, we will incorporate the more masculine aspects of ourselves and the Eastern teachings into our spiritual philosophy and practice.

3. *We foster the gifts of Western psychology, which provide us with the capacity of self-observation and the ability to remove unconscious blockages that hinder our*

right action in this world. That being said, we must keep in mind that psychology is but a tool meant to enable far more significant activities - it is definitely not our center of gravity! Thus, before anything else we're going to use the power of psychological observation to demolish the fears that drive us to clinging so badly to the psychological self-identity, and to discard the false need for endless healing and acceptance.

4. *We boldly proclaim the Guru's death, as an inevitable result of the external God's death* (God as an organizing, directing, grace-bestowing, order-giving force). In 'Guru's death' we don't mean that we no longer recognize the existence of higher inspiration and wisdom, but rather we mean the ending of any divine authority that one must obey and surrender to. *At*

the same time, we humbly acknowledge that this implies a far greater responsibility for our own individual journey. Individual sovereignty includes the duty of self-renunciation, self-liberation from all suffering and self-created morality. In the absence of external grace, we realize that self-effort is now the new grace, an evolutionary urge that can help man overcome himself.

5. *We declare the irrelevance of religious frameworks, along with their superstitions and beliefs, hopes and comforting ideas. We recognize that an authentic Western spirituality is a stripped-down transformative spirituality*, which stands alone and fully responsible, free from all belief and anticipation, grace and God's will, comforting concepts and fixed morality. It silently strives only to unveil

the naked true self which finally bursts from the depths of human evolution, glowing more powerfully than any mythological illuminated divine force.

6. *We profess a total commitment to engaging in the creative enterprise of the world and to being at the world's service until we breathe our last.* Out of the deepest possible realization that a Western spirituality - which constantly inhales objectivity and phenomena, direction and purpose, activism and clear stance - is the very opposite of narcissism, we take our stand in the midst of the world, choosing to be on the front lines of the evolutionary process and becoming the leading edge of world-changers. Spirituality, our own personal enlightenment included, is for the world, and anything less than that falls short. *In*

the full sense of the word, we are a social reform movement. To live up to this vision, we commit ourselves to fortifying our three lower chakras and aligning them with the higher.

7. *We will strive together to unionize all streams and schools of Western spirituality into one great and effective movement.* Without interfering with the sovereignty of each stream or obscuring the delicate differences between the various schools, our conviction is that only by unifying can we ever be able to undertake a challenge of this magnitude. Together we will overcome the tendency to overly differentiate and individualize, and we shall create a movement that will respond to the unconscious need of the world. We'll have our own democratic leadership, institutions and academies, schools and

congresses, scriptures and an ever-updating credo.

8. *We determine to use commerciality moderately, only in a way that will not corrupt the depths and thoroughgoing knowledge of our spirituality.* Though we will not avoid the many advantageous influences of Western capitalism, we will be always on the lookout to take care that this does not erode and weaken the less popular and the more demanding. We see no harm in allowing a more peripheral and featherweight spirituality, but *we'll keep the core of our movement flaring and glowing with the light of earth-shaking truths.*

9. *We will apply to our developing spirituality logical and scientific premises* (ceaseless destabilization of paradigm, developing

lineages, systematic coherence and the demand for evidence), knowing that this will enable us to both attain truthfulness and properly integrate into the Western culture. Together we will open ourselves to incorporating Western philosophies too into our emerging spirituality. *Above all, we will commit ourselves to consolidate a science of enlightenment*, that will draw from the extensive study of traditional wisdom and practice, but will also transcend them all towards a totally new paradigm of enlightenment.

10. *We shall wakefully explore the implications of natural evolution - the crumbling of all absolutes into the inner dynamics of the universe itself - for a new possible spiritual paradigm.* We realize that the most taken-for-granted spiritual premises might fall apart in the face of natural evolution. For

the time being, some influences can easily diffuse into our movement: a more complex non-duality that unifies matter and spirit; the understanding that we should not lean on some external force and shouldn't wait for anything to rescue us from above, and the thrilling understanding that consciousness is the most powerful resource not only in the context of personal liberation but also in the context of general evolution. Before anything else, we acknowledge that we are 2012 and any other world-changing date; that consciousness is the ultimate solution to the world's overwhelming problems, and so we are the grace we've been praying for from time immemorial.

Sources and inspirations

1. Swami Venkatesananda, *Yoga Vasishta*, State university of New York press, 1993

2. Walter Isaacson, *Einstein: his life and universe*, Simon & Schuster, 2008

3. Ken Wilber, A Spirituality That Transforms, *What is Enlightenment Magazine*, 1997

4. Beatrice Bruteau, A Song That Goes On Singing, *What is Enlightenment Magazine*, 2002

5. R.J. Hollingdale, Nietzsche: The Man and His Philosophy, *Cambridge University Press*, 1999

About the Author

Shai Tubali is the author of fourteen books in the Hebrew language, among them best-selling and prize-winning fiction and non-fiction.

He has been serving for the last twelve years as international lecturer and teacher (in Israel, Germany and India) in the field of spiritual transformation and spiritual therapy.

His knowledge of chakras and subtle anatomy is derived from learning in the Yogic Nityananda tradition through the American Yogi, Gabriel Cousens, M.D. It is also gathered from working with thousands of people in hundreds of workshops and sessions.

Shai Tubali is the developer of the White Light method, which enables people to utilize their subtle anatomy and chakras for the sake of psychological and spiritual balance.